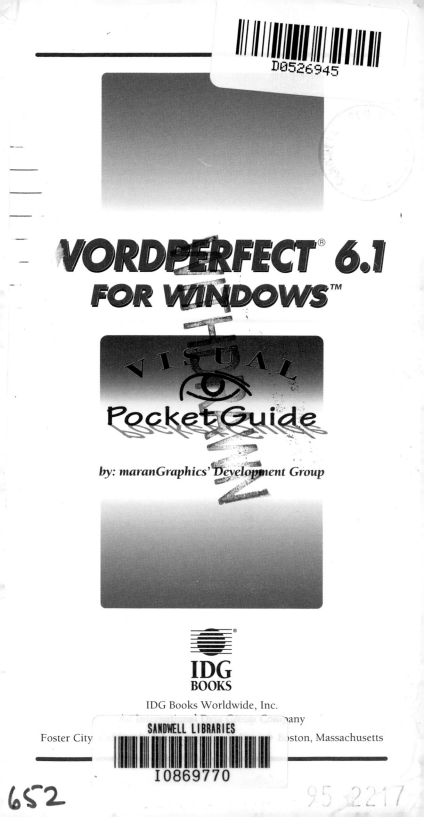

D0526945

VORDPERFECT® 6.1
FOR WINDOWS™

VISUAL
PocketGuide

by: maranGraphics' Development Group

IDG
BOOKS

IDG Books Worldwide, Inc.

An International Data Group Company

Foster City   Boston, Massachusetts

652
95 2217

WordPerfect® 6.1 for Windows™
Visual PocketGuide

Published by
IDG Books Worldwide, Inc.
An International Data Group Company
919 E. Hillsdale Blvd., Suite 400
Foster City, CA 94404
(415) 655-3000

Library of Congress Catalog Card No.: 95-075119

ISBN: 1-56884-668-1

Printed in the United States of America

10 9 8 7 6 5 4 3 2 1

Distributed in the United States by IDG Books Worldwide, Inc.

Distributed by Computer and Technical Books in Miami, Florida, for South America and the Caribbean; by Longman Singapore in Singapore, Malaysia, Thailand, and Korea; by Toppan Co. Ltd. in Japan; by IDG Communications HK in Hong Kong; by WoodsLane Pty. Ltd. in Australia and New Zealand; and by Transworld Publishers Ltd. in the U.K. and Europe.

For general information on IDG Books in the U.S., including information on discounts and premiums, contact IDG Books at 800-762-2974 or 317-895-5200.

For U.S. Corporate Sales and quantity discounts, contact maranGraphics at 800-469-6616, ext. 206.

For information on international sales of IDG Books, contact Helen Saraceni at 415-655-3021, Fax Number 415-655-3295.

For information on translations, contact Marc Jeffrey Mikulich, Director of Rights and Licensing, at IDG Books Worldwide. Fax Number 415-655-3295.

For sales inquiries and special prices for bulk quantities, write to the address above or call IDG Books Worldwide at 415-655-3000.

For information on using IDG Books in the classroom, or ordering examination copies, contact Jim Kelly at 800-434-2086.

TABLE OF CONTENTS

Format Pages

Working With Tables

A typewriter makes editing your document a difficult task. If you want to make minor changes, you have to use correction fluid. For extensive changes, you may have to retype your entire document.

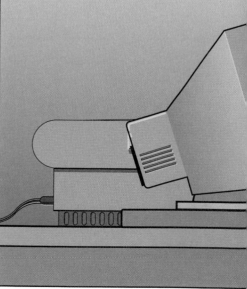

This is what you can create with WordPerfect for Windows.

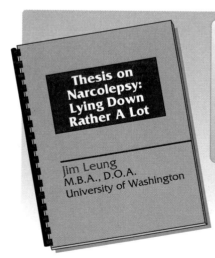

Thesis on Narcolepsy: Lying Down Rather A Lot

Jim Leung
M.B.A., D.O.A.
University of Washington

REPORTS AND MANUALS

WordPerfect for Windows provides editing and formatting features that make it ideal for producing longer documents such as reports and manuals.

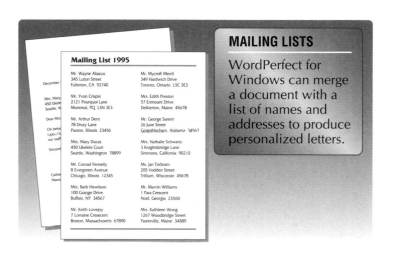

MAILING LISTS

WordPerfect for Windows can merge a document with a list of names and addresses to produce personalized letters.

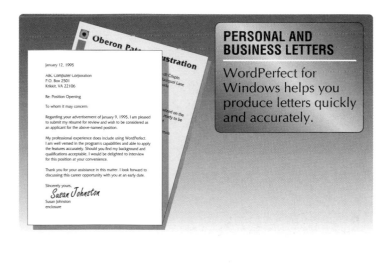

PERSONAL AND BUSINESS LETTERS

WordPerfect for Windows helps you produce letters quickly and accurately.

The mouse is a hand-held device that lets you quickly select commands and perform actions.

USING THE MOUSE

◆ Hold the mouse as shown in the diagram. Use your thumb and two rightmost fingers to guide the mouse while your two remaining fingers press the mouse buttons.

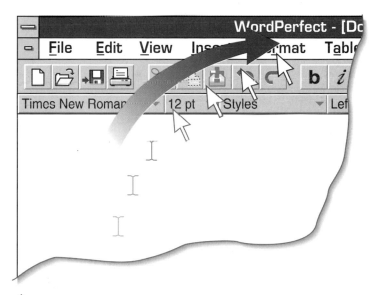

◆ When you move the mouse on your desk, the mouse pointer (I or $\searrow$) on your screen moves in the same direction. The mouse pointer changes shape depending on its location on your screen.

MOUSE BASICS

PARTS OF THE MOUSE

◆ The mouse has a left and right button. You can use these buttons to:

- open menus
- select commands
- choose options

Note: You will use the left button most of the time.

MOUSE TERMS

CLICK

Quickly press and release the left mouse button once.

DOUBLE-CLICK

Quickly press and release the left mouse button twice.

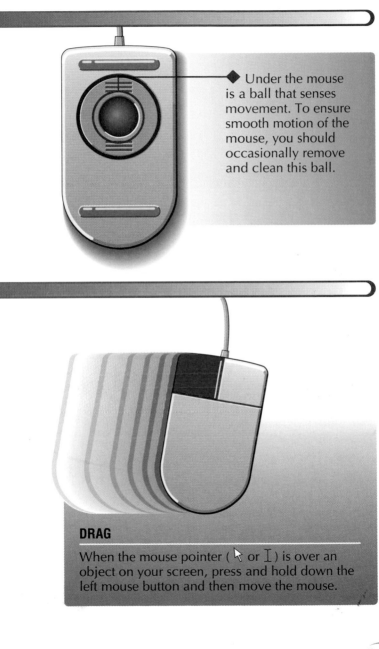

◆ Under the mouse is a ball that senses movement. To ensure smooth motion of the mouse, you should occasionally remove and clean this ball.

DRAG

When the mouse pointer (▸ or I) is over an object on your screen, press and hold down the left mouse button and then move the mouse.

START WORDPERFECT

START WORDPERFECT FOR WINDOWS

C:\> **WIN**

1 To start WordPerfect for Windows from MS-DOS, type **WIN** and then press Enter.

When you start WordPerfect for Windows, a blank document appears.

◆ The **Program Manager** window appears.

2 To open the **WPWin 6.1** group window, move the mouse ⬦ over this icon and then quickly press the left button twice.

To continue, refer to the next page.

START WORDPERFECT

Insert   HP DeskJet 500 (Win)   Select October 10, 1994   9:00AM Pg 1 Ln 1" Pos 1"

START WORDPERFECT (CONTINUED)

Program Manager

File   Options   Window   Help

WPWin 6.1

WordPerfect   Spell Checker   Thesaurus   QuickFinder   KickOff
                                          File Indexer

WPWin 6.1
Setup

Accessories   Games   StartUp   Main   Applications

◆ The **WPWin 6.1** group
window opens.

3 To start the **WordPerfect
for Windows** application,
move the mouse ⌖ over this
icon and then quickly press
the left button twice.

> You can type text into the document displayed on your screen.

◆ The **WordPerfect** window appears displaying a blank document.

◆ The flashing line on your screen indicates where the text you type will appear. It is called the **insertion point**.

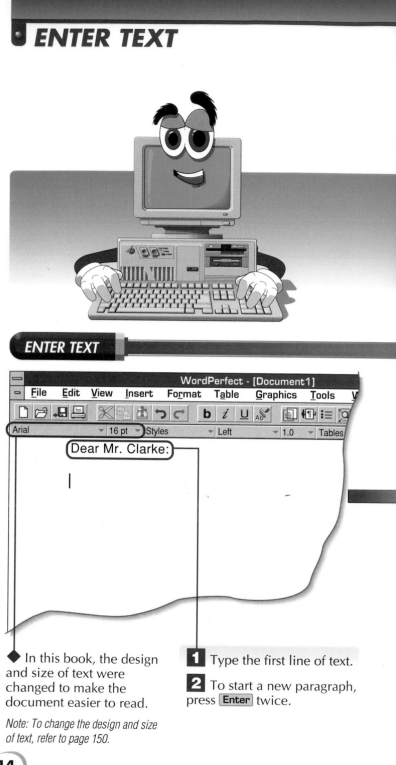

ENTER TEXT

WordPerfect - [Document1]

File   Edit   View   Insert   Format   Table   Graphics   Tools

Arial   16 pt   Styles   Left   1.0   Tables

Dear Mr. Clarke:

I

◆ In this book, the design and size of text were changed to make the document easier to read.

Note: To change the design and size of text, refer to page 150.

1 Type the first line of text.

2 To start a new paragraph, press **Enter** twice.

14

When typing text in your document, you do not need to press `Enter` at the end of a line. WordPerfect automatically moves the text to the next line. This is called word wrapping.

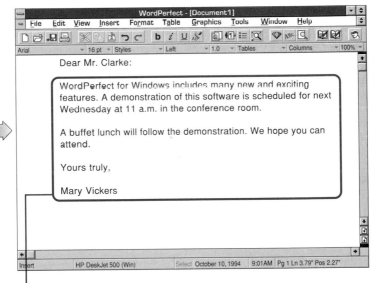

```
                    WordPerfect - [Document1]
  File  Edit  View  Insert  Format  Table  Graphics  Tools  Window  Help

Arial           16 pt   Styles        Left      1.0    Tables      Columns      100%

        Dear Mr. Clarke:

        WordPerfect for Windows includes many new and exciting
        features. A demonstration of this software is scheduled for next
        Wednesday at 11 a.m. in the conference room.

        A buffet lunch will follow the demonstration. We hope you can
        attend.

        Yours truly,

        Mary Vickers



  Insert     HP DeskJet 500 (Win)    Select October 10, 1994  9:01AM Pg 1 Ln 3.79" Pos 2.27"
```

3 Type the remaining text.

◆ Press `Enter` only when you want to start a new line or paragraph.

◆ To work faster in WordPerfect, display your document in the Draft mode.

Note: To change modes, refer to page 122.

15

THE STATUS BAR

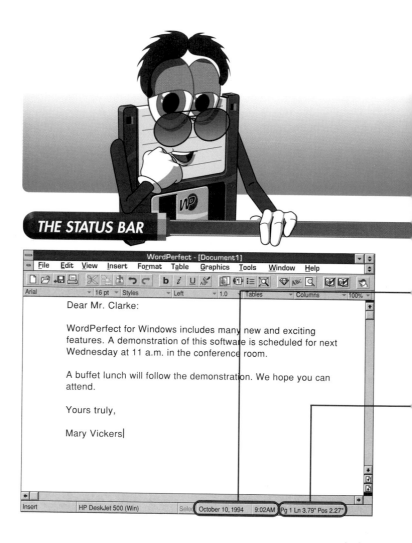

The Status bar displays the current date and time and the position of the insertion point in your document.

DATE AND TIME

This area displays the current date and time.

Note: If WordPerfect displays the wrong date or time, refer to your Windows manual to change the date or time set in your computer.

INSERTION POINT POSITION

This area displays the position of the insertion point in your document.

Pg 1
Identifies which page contains the insertion point.

Ln 3.79"
Defines how far (in inches) the insertion point is from the top of the page.

Pos 2.27"
Defines how far (in inches) the insertion point is from the left side of the page.

SELECT COMMANDS

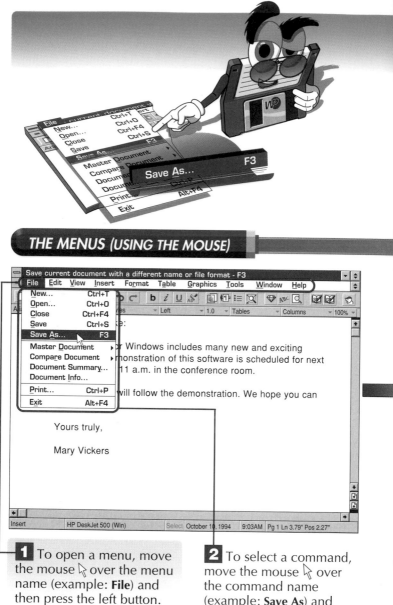

THE MENUS (USING THE MOUSE)

Save current document with a different name or file format - F3

File Edit View Insert Format Table Graphics Tools Window Help

New...	Ctrl+T
Open...	Ctrl+O
Close	Ctrl+F4
Save	Ctrl+S
Save As...	F3
Master Document	▸
Compare Document	▸
Document Summary...	
Document Info...	
Print...	Ctrl+P
Exit	Alt+F4

b i U

Left   1.0   Tables   Columns   100%

e:

r Windows includes many new and exciting
onstration of this software is scheduled for next
11 a.m. in the conference room.

will follow the demonstration. We hope you can

Yours truly,

Mary Vickers

Insert   HP DeskJet 500 (Win)   Select October 10, 1994   9:03AM Pg 1 Ln 3.79" Pos 2.27"

1 To open a menu, move the mouse ⌖ over the menu name (example: **File**) and then press the left button.

Note: To close a menu, move the mouse ⌖ outside the menu and then press the left button.

2 To select a command, move the mouse ⌖ over the command name (example: **Save As**) and then press the left button.

18

You can open a menu to display a list of related commands. You can then select the command you want to use.

		WordPerfect - [Document1]			
File	Edit	View	Insert	For̲mat	Table	Graphics	Tools	Window	Help

Save As

Filena̲me:
c:\office\wpwin\wpdocs

OK

Cancel

QuickList:

sample.wpd
tourgmk.wpd

Documents
Graphics Directory
Macro Directory
Printer Directory
Template Directory

View...

QuickFinder...

File Options ▾

QuickList ▾

Directories:

c:\
office
wpwin
wpdocs

Setup...

Help

Total Files: 2
Total Bytes: 7,023
Sort: Filename Ascending

Drives: 15,534 KB Free

c:

Save File as T̲ype: WordPerfect 6.0/6.1 [*.wpd; * .wpt; * .doc]

☐ Password Protect

Insert   HP DeskJet 500 (Win)   Select October 10, 1994   9:04AM   Pg 1 Ln 3.79" Pos 2.27"

◆ A dialog box appears if WordPerfect requires more information to carry out the command.

3 To close a dialog box, move the mouse ⌖ over **Cancel** or **Close** and then press the left button.

19

SELECT COMMANDS

You can use the keyboard to select a command.

THE MENUS (USING THE KEYBOARD)

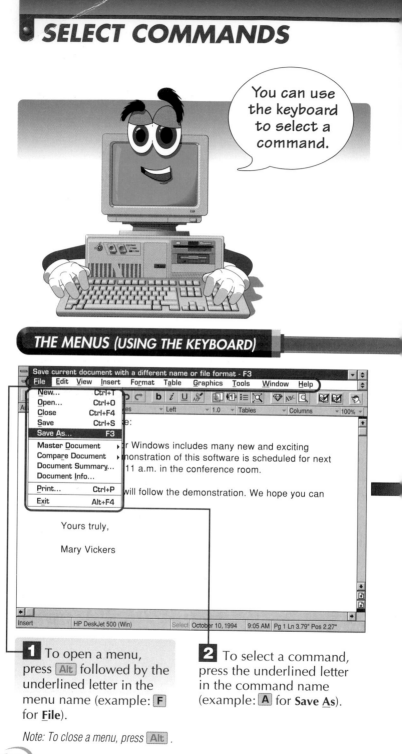

Save current document with a different name or file format - F3

File Edit View Insert Format Table Graphics Tools Window Help

New...   Ctrl+T
Open...   Ctrl+O
Close   Ctrl+F4
Save   Ctrl+S
Save As...   F3
Master Document   ▸
Compare Document   ▸
Document Summary...
Document Info...
Print...   Ctrl+P
Exit   Alt+F4

es   ▾ Left   ▾ 1.0   ▾ Tables   ▾ Columns   ▾ 100% ▾

e:

r Windows includes many new and exciting
onstration of this software is scheduled for next
11 a.m. in the conference room.

will follow the demonstration. We hope you can

Yours truly,

Mary Vickers

Insert   HP DeskJet 500 (Win)   Select October 10, 1994   9:05 AM Pg 1 Ln 3.79" Pos 2.27"

1 To open a menu, press **Alt** followed by the underlined letter in the menu name (example: **F** for **File**).

*Note: To close a menu, press **Alt** .*

2 To select a command, press the underlined letter in the command name (example: **A** for **Save As**).

20

TIP

Edit

Undo	**Ctrl+Z**
Redo	Ctrl+Shift+R
Undo/Redo History...	
Undelete...	Ctrl+Shift+Z
Repeat...	
Cut	Ctrl+X
Copy	Ctrl+C
Paste	Ctrl+V
Append	

◆ *If a command name is dimmed (example: Cut), it is currently unavailable.*

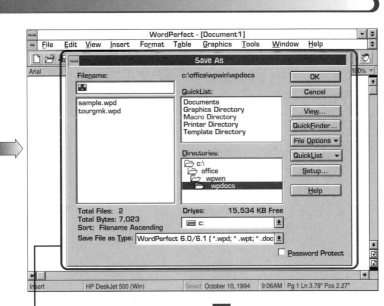

◆ A dialog box appears if WordPerfect requires more information to carry out the command.

3 To close a dialog box, press **Esc**.

21

SELECT COMMANDS

THE WORDPERFECT BUTTONS

Each button displayed on your screen provides a fast method of selecting a menu command.

For example, you can use 🖫 to quickly select the Save command.

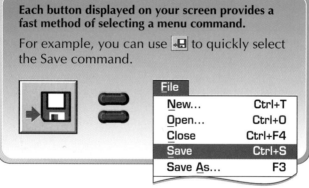

File	
New...	Ctrl+T
Open...	Ctrl+O
Close	Ctrl+F4
Save	Ctrl+S
Save **A**s...	F3

You can use the WordPerfect buttons to quickly select the most commonly used commands.

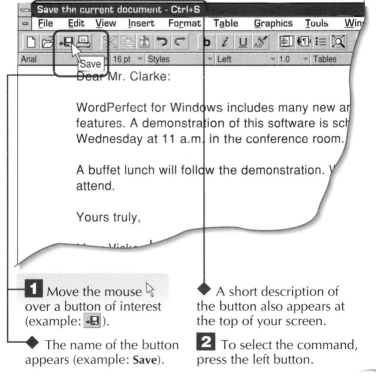

1 Move the mouse over a button of interest (example:).

◆ The name of the button appears (example: **Save**).

◆ A short description of the button also appears at the top of your screen.

2 To select the command, press the left button.

23

Styles
Left
Mr. Clarke:
WordPerfect for Windows includes ma
features
of this softwa
Wednesd
he conference
Cut
Copy
Paste
Delete
Font...
QuickFormat...
Spell Check...
Reveal Codes
Bullets...
e demonstratio

THE QUICKMENUS

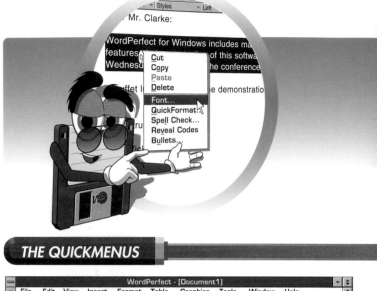

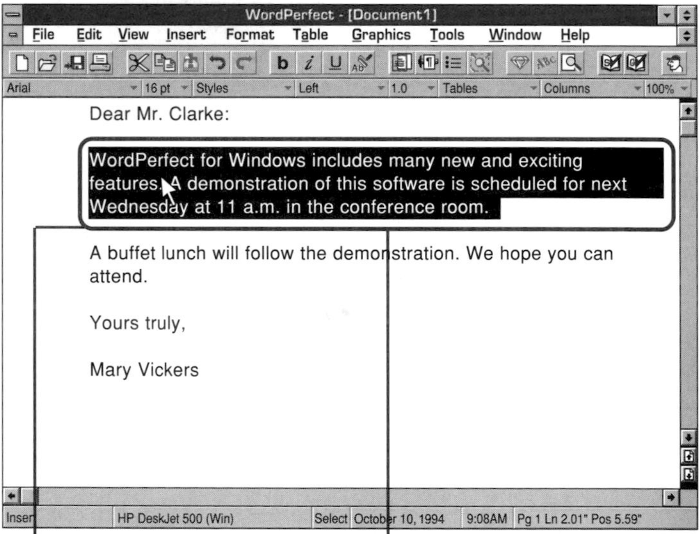
WordPerfect - [Document1]
File Edit View Insert Format Table Graphics Tools Window Help
Arial 16 pt Styles Left 1.0 Tables Columns 100%
Dear Mr. Clarke:
WordPerfect for Windows includes many new and exciting features. A demonstration of this software is scheduled for next Wednesday at 11 a.m. in the conference room.
A buffet lunch will follow the demonstration. We hope you can attend.
Yours truly,
Mary Vickers
HP DeskJet 500 (Win)
Select October 10, 1994 9:08AM Pg 1 Ln 2.01" Pos 5.59"

1 Select the text you want to work with.

Note: To select text, refer to page 30.

2 Move the mouse anywhere over the text you selected and then press the **right** button.

A QuickMenu
displays a list
of commonly used
commands that you
can apply to text
you select.

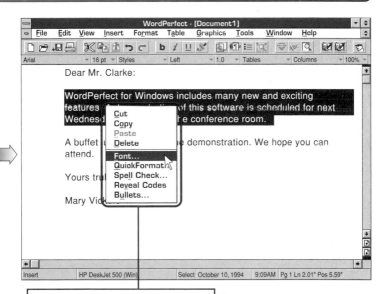

◆ A QuickMenu appears.

Note: You can display a QuickMenu over selected text or any other area on your screen.

3 Move the mouse ▷ over the command you want to use and then press the left button.

Note: To close the QuickMenu, move the mouse ▷ outside the menu and then press the left button.

MOVE THROUGH A DOCUMENT

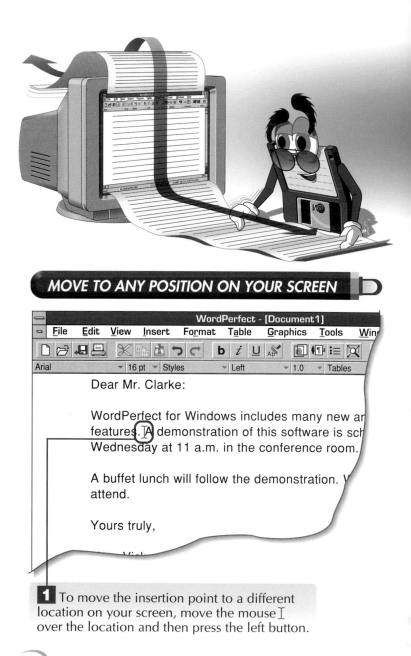

MOVE TO ANY POSITION ON YOUR SCREEN

WordPerfect - [Document1]

| File | Edit | View | Insert | Format | Table | Graphics | Tools | Win |

Arial ▾ 16 pt ▾ Styles ▾ Left ▾ 1.0 ▾ Tables

Dear Mr. Clarke:

WordPerfect for Windows includes many new an features. A demonstration of this software is sch Wednesday at 11 a.m. in the conference room.

A buffet lunch will follow the demonstration. attend.

Yours truly,

1 To move the insertion point to a different location on your screen, move the mouse I over the location and then press the left button.

If you create a long document, your computer screen cannot display all the text at the same time. You must move through the document to view other areas of text.

VIEW PREVIOUS OR NEXT PAGE

If your document contains more than one page, you can view the previous or next page.

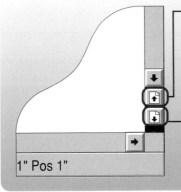

◆ To view the previous page, move the mouse over and then press the left button.

◆ To view the next page, move the mouse over and then press the left button.

1" Pos 1"

MOVE THROUGH A DOCUMENT

SCROLL UP OR DOWN

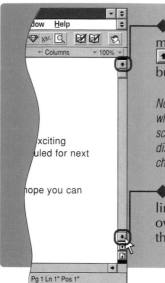

◆ To scroll up one line, move the mouse ⋉ over ⬆ and then press the left button.

*Note: You can only scroll up or down when your text extends beyond one screen **or** when your document is displayed in the Page mode. To change modes, refer to page 122.*

◆ To scroll down one line, move the mouse ⋉ over ⬇ and then press the left button.

KEYBOARD SHORTCUTS

◆ Press this key to move the insertion point **up** one line.

◆ Press this key to move the insertion point **right** one character.

◆ Press this key to move the insertion point **left** one character.

◆ Press this key to move the insertion point **down** one line.

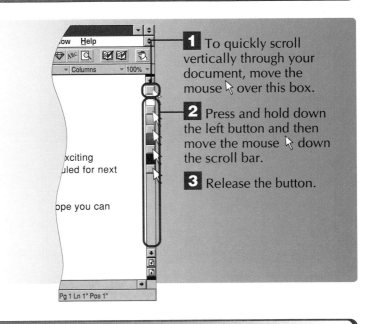

1 To quickly scroll vertically through your document, move the mouse ⩗ over this box.

2 Press and hold down the left button and then move the mouse ⩗ down the scroll bar.

3 Release the button.

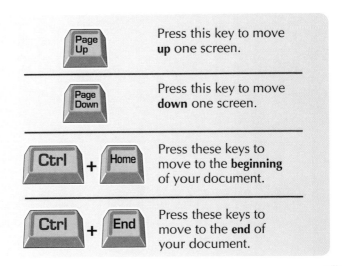

Page Up	Press this key to move **up** one screen.
Page Down	Press this key to move **down** one screen.
Ctrl + Home	Press these keys to move to the **beginning** of your document.
Ctrl + End	Press these keys to move to the **end** of your document.

SELECT TEXT

SELECT A WORD

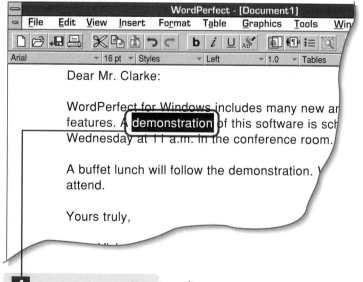

```
                    WordPerfect - [Document1]
  File   Edit   View   Insert   Format   Table   Graphics   Tools   Win
```

Dear Mr. Clarke:

WordPerfect for Windows includes many new an
features. A demonstration of this software is sch
Wednesday at 11 a.m. in the conference room.

A buffet lunch will follow the demonstration.
attend.

Yours truly,

1 Move the mouse I anywhere over the word you want to select and then quickly press the left button **twice**.

◆ To cancel a text selection, move the mouse I anywhere outside the selected area and then press the left button.

Before you
can use many
WordPerfect features,
you must first select
the text you want
to change.

SELECT A SENTENCE

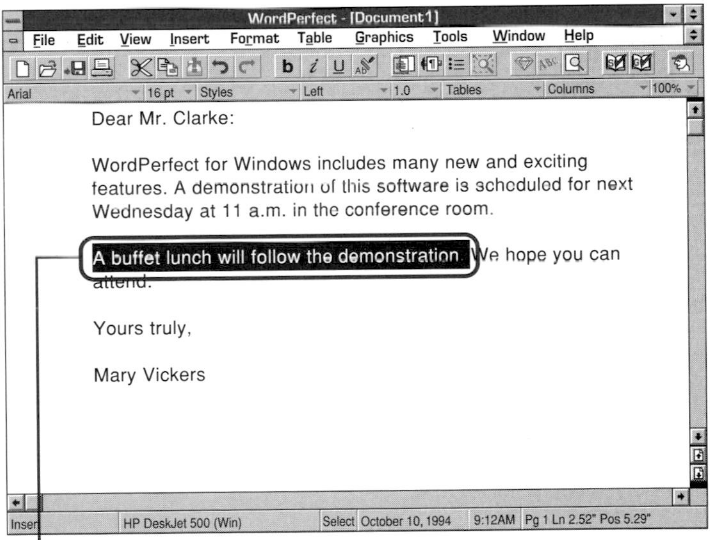
WordPerfect - [Document1]
File Edit View Insert Format Table Graphics Tools Window Help
Arial 16 pt Styles Left 1.0 Tables Columns 100%
Dear Mr. Clarke:
WordPerfect for Windows includes many new and exciting features. A demonstration of this software is scheduled for next Wednesday at 11 a.m. in the conference room.
A buffet lunch will follow the demonstration. We hope you can attend.
Yours truly,
Mary Vickers
HP DeskJet 500 (Win)
Select October 10, 1994 9:12AM Pg 1 Ln 2.52" Pos 5.29"

1 Move the mouse I anywhere over the sentence you want to select and then quickly press the left button **three** times.

SELECT A PARAGRAPH

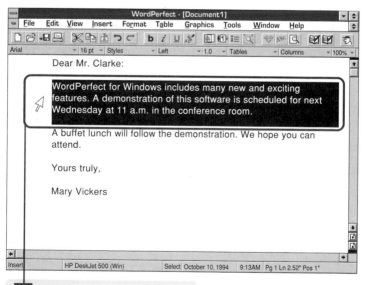

1 Move the mouse I to the left of the paragraph you want to select (I changes to ↗) and then quickly press the left button twice.

◆ To cancel a text selection, move the mouse I anywhere outside the selected area and then press the left button.

Selected text appears highlighted on your screen.

SELECT ANY AMOUNT OF TEXT

WordPerfect - [Document.1]

File Edit View Insert Format Table Graphics Tools Win

Arial   16 pt   Styles   Left   1.0   Tables

Dear Mr. Clarke:

WordPerfect for Windows includes many new an
features. A demonstration of this software is sch
Wednesday at 11 a.m. in the conference room.

A buffet lunch will follow the demonstration.
attend.

Yours truly,

1 Move the mouse over the first word you want to select.

2 Press and hold down the left button as you drag the mouse over the text. Then release the button.

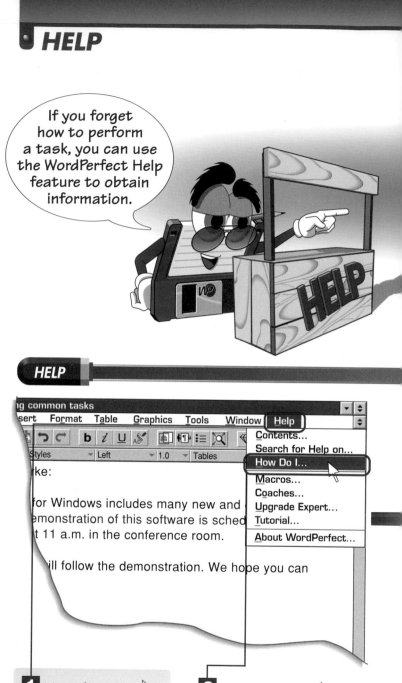

If you forget how to perform a task, you can use the WordPerfect Help feature to obtain information.

HELP

ng common tasks

sert Format Table Graphics Tools Window Help

Styles Left 1.0 Tables

ke:

Contents...
Search for Help on...
How Do I...

Macros...
Coaches...
Upgrade Expert...
Tutorial...

About WordPerfect...

for Windows includes many new and
emonstration of this software is sched
t 11 a.m. in the conference room.

ill follow the demonstration. We hope you can

1 Move the mouse ⩗ over **Help** and then press the left button.

2 Move the mouse ⩗ over **How Do I** and then press the left button.

◆ The **Indexes** window appears displaying a list of help topics.

3 Move the mouse 🖑 over a topic of interest (example: **Create Documents**) and then press the left button.

To continue, refer to the next page.

HELP

The Help feature can save you time by eliminating the need to refer to other sources.

Indexes
How Do I
📖 Open Books   📕 Close Books   Close
📖 **Create Documents**
▤ My First Documents
▤ Personal/Business Documents
▤ Papers, Books, Reports
▤ Forms
📕 Open and Save Documents
📕 Create/Edit Text
📕 Format Document
📕 Add Pictures, Graphics, Sound
📕 Print Documents
📕 Use Time-Saving Features
📕 Customize WordPerfect
📕 Send, Link, Launch, and Import

Document1]

Graphics   Tools   Window   Help

▾ 1.0   ▾ Tables   ▾ Columns   ▾ 100% ▾

…des many new and exciting …is software is scheduled for next …nference room.

…monstration. We hope you can

October 10, 1994   9:17AM   Pg 1 Ln 4.04" Pos 1"

◆ A list of subtopics appears.

4 Move the mouse 🖑 over a subtopic of interest (example: **My First Documents**) and then press the left button.

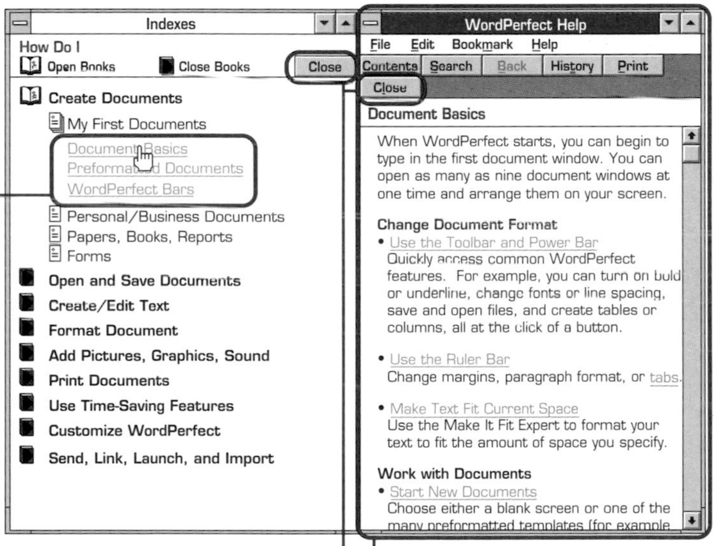

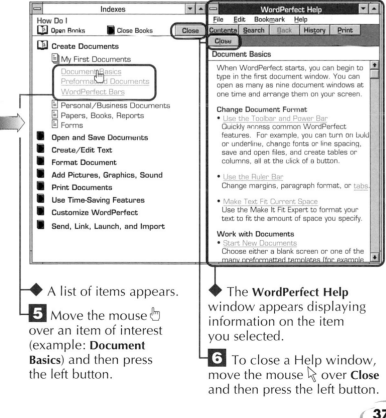

◆ A list of items appears.

5 Move the mouse over an item of interest (example: **Document Basics**) and then press the left button.

◆ The **WordPerfect Help** window appears displaying information on the item you selected.

6 To close a Help window, move the mouse over **Close** and then press the left button.

INSERT A BLANK LINE

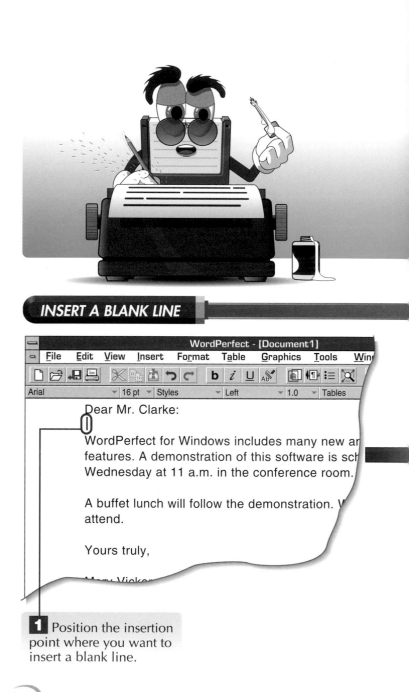

INSERT A BLANK LINE

1 Position the insertion point where you want to insert a blank line.

WordPerfect makes it easy to edit your document. To make changes, you no longer have to retype a page or use correction fluid.

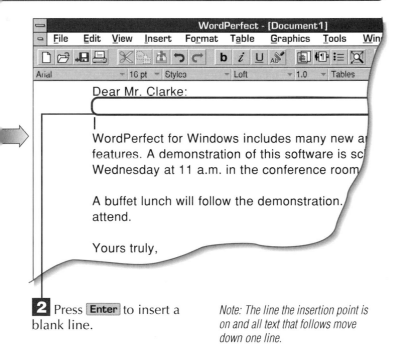

WordPerfect - [Document1]

File   Edit   View   Insert   Format   Table   Graphics   Tools   Win

Arial   16 pt   Styles   Left   1.0   Tables

Dear Mr. Clarke:

WordPerfect for Windows includes many new a
features. A demonstration of this software is sc
Wednesday at 11 a.m. in the conference room

A buffet lunch will follow the demonstration.
attend.

Yours truly,

2 Press **Enter** to insert a blank line.

Note: The line the insertion point is on and all text that follows move down one line.

SPLIT AND JOIN PARAGRAPHS

You can easily split and join paragraphs in your document.

SPLIT AND JOIN PARAGRAPHS

WordPerfect - [Document1]

File Edit View Insert Format Table Graphics Tools Win

Arial   16 pt   Styles   Left   1.0   Tables

Dear Mr. Clarke:

WordPerfect for Windows includes many new a features A demonstration of this software is sc Wednesday at 11 a.m. in the conference room

A buffet lunch will follow the demonstration. attend.

Yours truly,

Split a Paragraph

1 Position the insertion point where you want to split a paragraph in two.

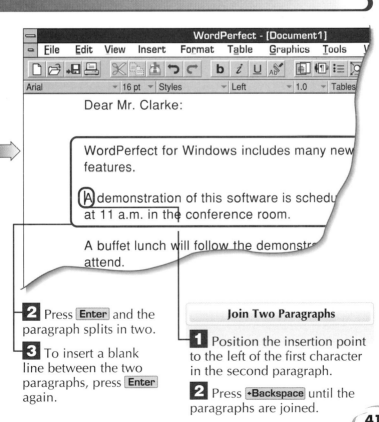

Dear Mr. Clarke:

WordPerfect for Windows includes many new features.

A demonstration of this software is schedu at 11 a.m. in the conference room.

A buffet lunch will follow the demonstra attend.

2 Press **Enter** and the paragraph splits in two.

3 To insert a blank line between the two paragraphs, press **Enter** again.

Join Two Paragraphs

1 Position the insertion point to the left of the first character in the second paragraph.

2 Press **Backspace** until the paragraphs are joined.

INSERT TEXT

In the Insert mode, the text you type appears at the insertion point location. The existing text moves forward to make room for the new text.

INSERT TEXT

WordPerfect - [Document1]

File   Edit   View   Insert   Format   Table   Graphics   Tools   Window   Help

Arial   16 pt   Styles   Left   1.0   Tables   Columns   100%

Dear Mr. Clarke:

WordPerfect for Windows includes many new and exciting features. A demonstration of this software is scheduled for next Wednesday at 11 a.m. in the conference room.

A buffet lunch will follow the demonstration. We hope you can attend.

Yours truly,

Mary Vickers

Insert   HP DeskJet 500 (Win)   Select October 10, 1994   9:23AM   Pg 1 Ln 2.01" Pos 2.13"

When you start WordPerfect, the program is in the Insert mode.

1 Position the insertion point where you want to insert the new text.

◆ If the word **Typeover** is displayed at the bottom of your screen, press Insert. This turns on the **Insert** mode.

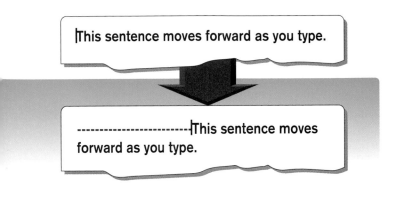

This sentence moves forward as you type.

-------------------------This sentence moves forward as you type.

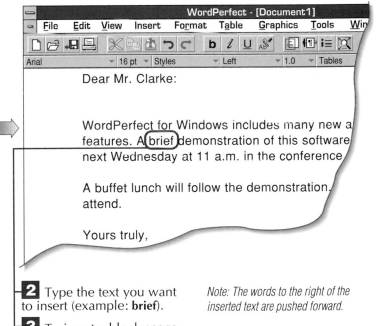

WordPerfect - [Document1]

File   Edit   View   Insert   Format   Table   Graphics   Tools   Win

Arial   ▾ 16 pt ▾ Styles   ▾ Left   ▾ 1.0   ▾ Tables

Dear Mr. Clarke:

WordPerfect for Windows includes many new a
features. A brief demonstration of this software
next Wednesday at 11 a.m. in the conference

A buffet lunch will follow the demonstration.
attend.

Yours truly,

2 Type the text you want to insert (example: **brief**).

3 To insert a blank space, press the **Spacebar**.

Note: The words to the right of the inserted text are pushed forward.

43

> In the Typeover mode, the text you type appears at the insertion point location. The new text replaces (types over) any existing text.

TYPEOVER TEXT

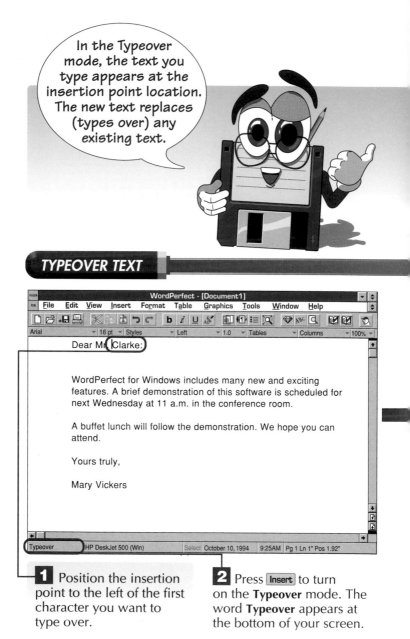

1 Position the insertion point to the left of the first character you want to type over.

2 Press **Insert** to turn on the **Typeover** mode. The word **Typeover** appears at the bottom of your screen.

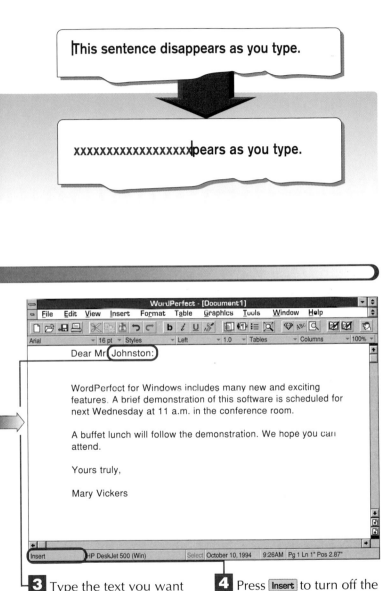

This sentence disappears as you type.

xxxxxxxxxxxxxxxxxxxxpears as you type.

3 Type the text you want to replace the existing text (example: **Johnston:**).

4 Press **Insert** to turn off the **Typeover** mode. The word **Insert** appears at the bottom of your screen.

DELETE CHARACTERS

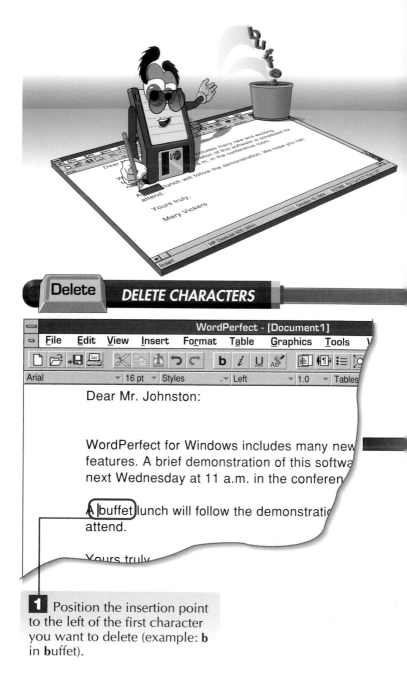

Delete **DELETE CHARACTERS**

WordPerfect - [Document1]

File   Edit   View   Insert   Format   Table   Graphics   Tools

Arial   16 pt   Styles   Left   1.0   Tables

Dear Mr. Johnston:

WordPerfect for Windows includes many new
features. A brief demonstration of this softwa
next Wednesday at 11 a.m. in the conferen

A buffet lunch will follow the demonstratio
attend.

Yours truly

1 Position the insertion point
to the left of the first character
you want to delete (example: **b**
in **b**uffet).

46

You can use
Delete to remove the
character to the right of
the insertion point. The
remaining text moves
to the left.

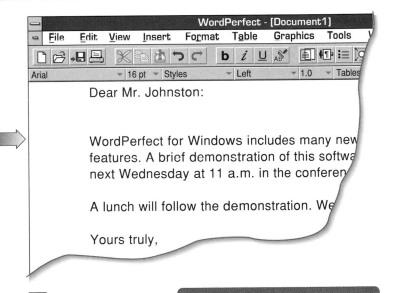

2 Press Delete once
for each character
or space you want
to delete (example:
press Delete seven
times).

You can also use
this key to delete
characters. Position
the insertion point to the **right**
of the character(s) you want to
delete and then press Backspace.

47

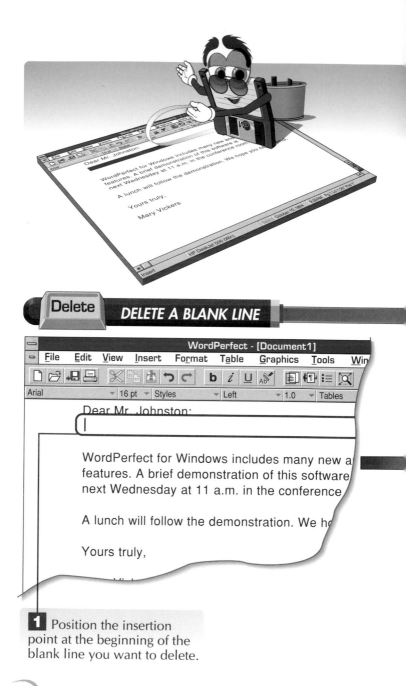

Delete   **DELETE A BLANK LINE**

1 Position the insertion point at the beginning of the blank line you want to delete.

You can use
Delete to remove the
blank line the insertion
point is on. The remaining
text moves up
one line.

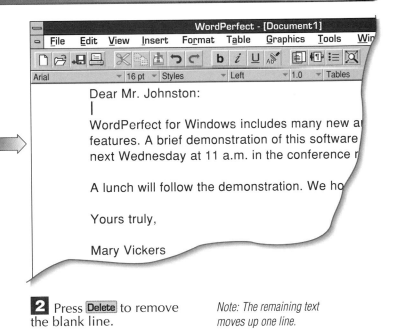

2 Press Delete to remove
the blank line.

*Note: The remaining text
moves up one line.*

DELETE SELECTED TEXT

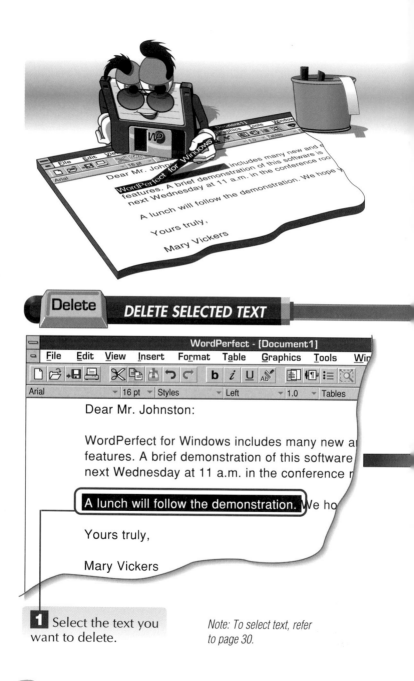

Delete

DELETE SELECTED TEXT

WordPerfect - [Document1]

File   Edit   View   Insert   Format   Table   Graphics   Tools   Win

Arial   16 pt   Styles   Left   1.0   Tables

Dear Mr. Johnston:

WordPerfect for Windows includes many new a
features. A brief demonstration of this software
next Wednesday at 11 a.m. in the conference

A lunch will follow the demonstration. We ho

Yours truly,

Mary Vickers

1 Select the text you want to delete.

Note: To select text, refer to page 30.

You can use
Delete to remove text
you have selected. The
remaining text moves up
or to the left to fill the
empty space.

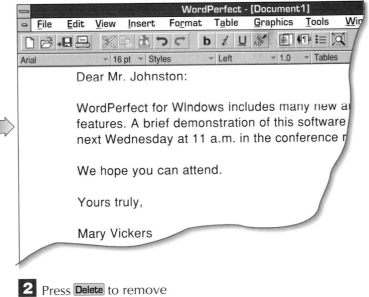

WordPerfect - [Document1]

File   Edit   View   Insert   Format   Table   Graphics   Tools   Win

Arial   ▾ 16 pt ▾ Styles   ▾ Left   ▾ 1.0   ▾ Tables

Dear Mr. Johnston:

WordPerfect for WIndows includes many new a
features. A brief demonstration of this software
next Wednesday at 11 a.m. in the conference r

We hope you can attend.

Yours truly,

Mary Vickers

2 Press Delete to remove
the text.

UNDO LAST CHANGES

UNDO LAST CHANGES

Reverse the last change made to the document - Ctrl+Z

File Edit View Insert Format Table Graphics Tools Win

Arial   ▼ 16 pt ▼ Styles   ▼ Left   ▼ 1.0 ▼ Tables

Dear Mr. Johnston:

WordPerfect for Windows includes many new ar
features. A brief demonstration of this software
next Wednesday at 11 a.m. in the conference ro

We hope you can attend.

Yours truly,

Mary Vickers

1 Move the mouse ▢
over ⟲ and then press
the left button.

*Note: The Undo feature can
cancel your last editing and
formatting changes.*

> WordPerfect remembers the last changes you made to your document. If you regret these changes, you can cancel them by using the Undo feature.

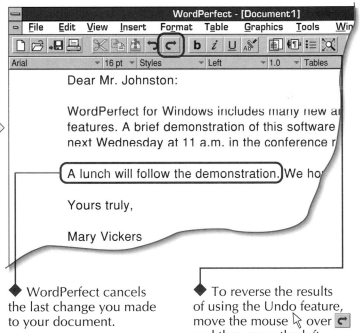

Dear Mr. Johnston:

WordPerfect for Windows includes many new a[...] features. A brief demonstration of this software [...] next Wednesday at 11 a.m. in the conference r[...]

A lunch will follow the demonstration. We ho[...]

Yours truly,

Mary Vickers

◆ WordPerfect cancels the last change you made to your document.

◆ Repeat step **1** to cancel previous changes you made.

◆ To reverse the results of using the Undo feature, move the mouse ⌖ over ⟳ and then press the left button.

53

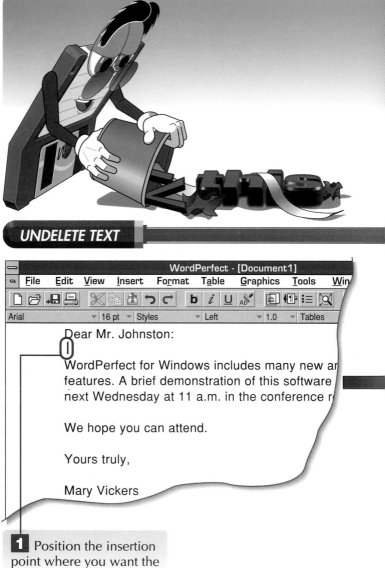

UNDELETE TEXT

WordPerfect - [Document1]

| File | Edit | View | Insert | Format | Table | Graphics | Tools | Win |

Arial — 16 pt — Styles — Left — 1.0 — Tables

Dear Mr. Johnston:

WordPerfect for Windows includes many new an
features. A brief demonstration of this software
next Wednesday at 11 a.m. in the conference r

We hope you can attend.

Yours truly,

Mary Vickers

1 Position the insertion point where you want the deleted text to reappear.

If you accidentally delete text, you can use the Undelete feature to restore the text.

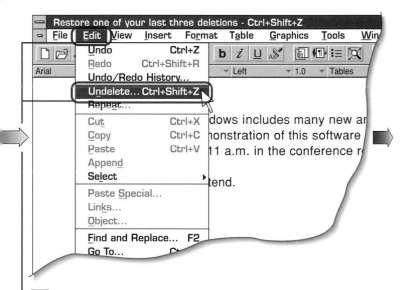

Restore one of your last three deletions - Ctrl+Shift+Z

File | Edit | View | Insert | Format | Table | Graphics | Tools | Win

Undo — Ctrl+Z
Redo — Ctrl+Shift+R
Undo/Redo History...
Undelete... Ctrl+Shift+Z
Repeat...
Cut — Ctrl+X
Copy — Ctrl+C
Paste — Ctrl+V
Append
Select ▸
Paste Special...
Links...
Object...
Find and Replace... F2
Go To...

Arial — Left — 1.0 — Tables

dows includes many new an
onstration of this software
11 a.m. in the conference r

tend.

2 Move the mouse ⊳ over **Edit** and then press the left button.

3 Move the mouse ⊳ over **Undelete** and then press the left button.

◆ The **Undelete** dialog box appears.

To continue, refer to the next page.

55

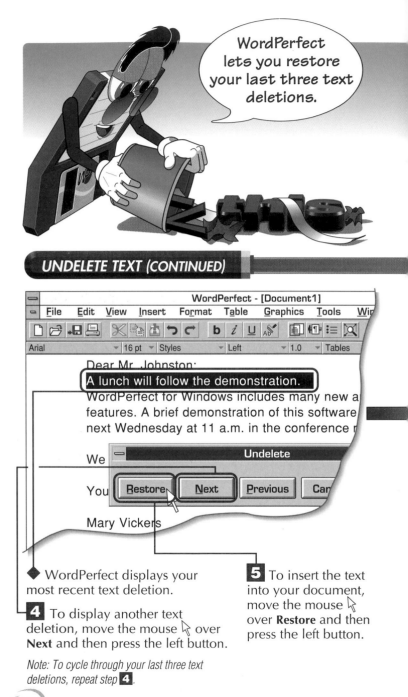

WordPerfect lets you restore your last three text deletions.

UNDELETE TEXT (CONTINUED)

◆ WordPerfect displays your most recent text deletion.

4 To display another text deletion, move the mouse � over **Next** and then press the left button.

Note: To cycle through your last three text deletions, repeat step **4**.

5 To insert the text into your document, move the mouse ⊠ over **Restore** and then press the left button.

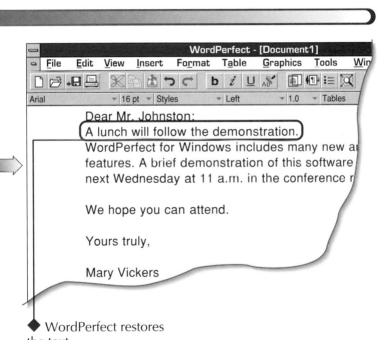

◆ WordPerfect restores
the text.

MOVE TEXT

DRAG AND DROP TEXT

WordPerfect - [Document1]

File Edit View Insert Format Table Graphics Tools Win

Arial   ▼ 16 pt ▼ Styles   ▼ Left   ▼ 1.0 ▼ Tables

Dear Mr. Johnston:

A lunch will follow the demonstration.

WordPerfect for Windows includes many new ar
features. A brief demonstration of this software
next Wednesday at 11 a.m. in the conference r

We hope you can attend.

Yours truly,

Mary Vickers

1 Select the text you want to move.

Note: To select text, refer to page 30.

2 Move the mouse I anywhere over the selected text and I changes to ⌖.

3 Press and hold down the left button as you drag the mouse ⌖ to where you want to place the text.

Note: The text will appear where the insertion point flashes on your screen.

You can move text from one location in your document to another.

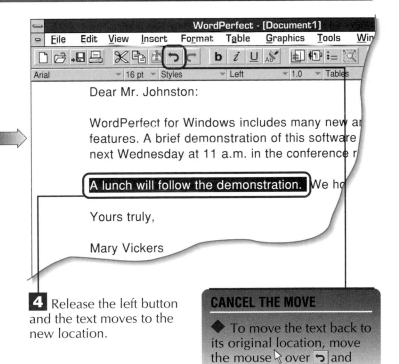

4 Release the left button and the text moves to the new location.

CANCEL THE MOVE

◆ To move the text back to its original location, move the mouse ▷ over ⤴ and then press the left button.

MOVE TEXT

CUT AND PASTE TEXT

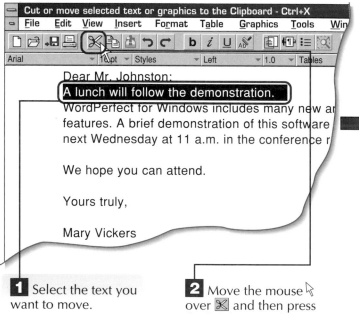

Cut or move selected text or graphics to the Clipboard - Ctrl+X

File   Edit   View   Insert   Format   Table   Graphics   Tools   Win

Arial   16pt   Styles   Left   1.0   Tables

Dear Mr. Johnston:

A lunch will follow the demonstration.

WordPerfect for Windows includes many new an
features. A brief demonstration of this software
next Wednesday at 11 a.m. in the conference r

We hope you can attend.

Yours truly,

Mary Vickers

1 Select the text you want to move.

Note: To select text, refer to page 30.

2 Move the mouse ⌖ over ✂ and then press the left button. The text you selected disappears from your screen.

You can use
the Cut and Paste
buttons to move text
to a new location in
your document.

Insert the Clipboard contents at the insertion point - Ctrl+V

File   Edit   View   Insert   Format   Table   Graphics   Tools   Win

Arial   ▾ 16 pt ▾ Styles   ▾ Left   ▾ 1.0   ▾ Tables

Dear Mr. Johnston:

WordPerfect for Windows includes many new a
features. A brief demonstration of this software
next Wednesday at 11 a.m. in the conference r

A lunch will follow the demonstration.   We h

Yours truly,

Mary Vickers

3 Position the insertion
point where you want to
place the text.

4 Move the mouse ⌖
over 🖪 and then press
the left button.

◆ The text moves to the
new location.

COPY TEXT

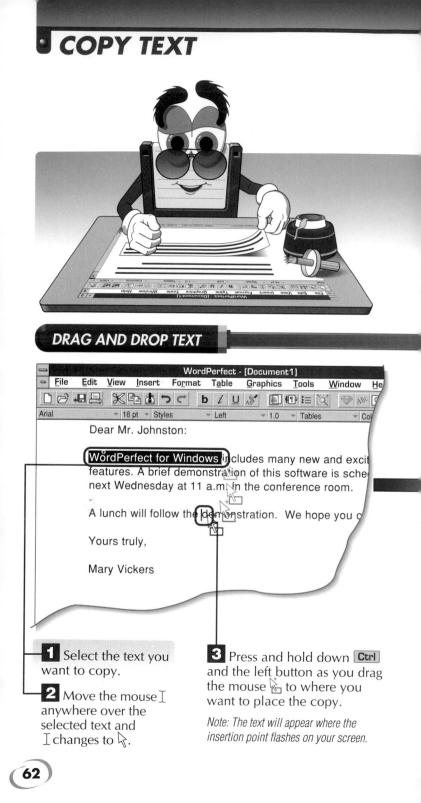

DRAG AND DROP TEXT

WordPerfect - [Document1]

File Edit View Insert Format Table Graphics Tools Window He

Arial   16 pt   Styles   Left   1.0   Tables   Col

Dear Mr. Johnston:

WordPerfect for Windows includes many new and excit
features. A brief demonstration of this software is sche
next Wednesday at 11 a.m. in the conference room.

A lunch will follow the demonstration. We hope you c

Yours truly,

Mary Vickers

1 Select the text you want to copy.

2 Move the mouse I anywhere over the selected text and I changes to ↖.

3 Press and hold down Ctrl and the left button as you drag the mouse ↖ to where you want to place the copy.

Note: The text will appear where the insertion point flashes on your screen.

62

You can copy text and then place the copy in a new location. This will save you time since you do not have to retype the text.

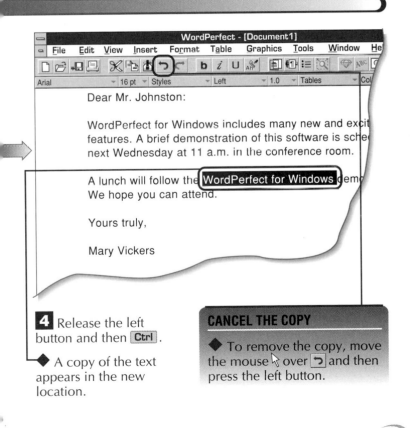

4 Release the left button and then **Ctrl**.

◆ A copy of the text appears in the new location.

CANCEL THE COPY

◆ To remove the copy, move the mouse ⬚ over ⤺ and then press the left button.

COPY TEXT

COPY AND PASTE TEXT

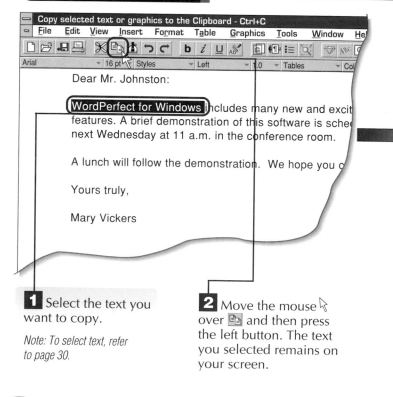

Copy selected text or graphics to the Clipboard - Ctrl+C

File　Edit　View　Insert　Format　Table　Graphics　Tools　Window　He

Arial　　　16 pt　Styles　　Left　　1.0　Tables　　Col

Dear Mr. Johnston:

WordPerfect for Windows includes many new and excit
features. A brief demonstration of this software is sche
next Wednesday at 11 a.m. in the conference room.

A lunch will follow the demonstration. We hope you c

Yours truly,

Mary Vickers

1 Select the text you want to copy.

Note: To select text, refer to page 30.

2 Move the mouse ⤹ over 🖺 and then press the left button. The text you selected remains on your screen.

You can use the Copy and Paste buttons to place a copy of text in a new location.

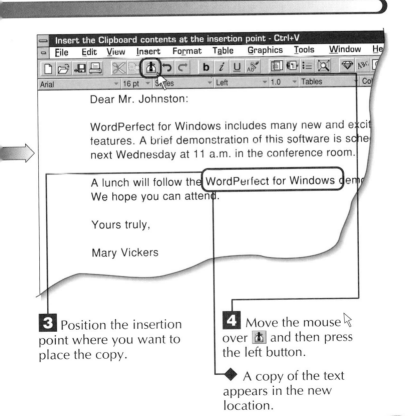

3 Position the insertion point where you want to place the copy.

4 Move the mouse over 📄 and then press the left button.

◆ A copy of the text appears in the new location.

65

CHANGE THE CASE OF TEXT

You can change the case of text in your document without having to retype the text.

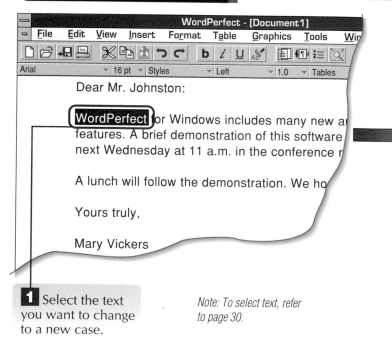

```
                    WordPerfect - [Document1]
File   Edit   View   Insert   Format   Table   Graphics   Tools   Win
Arial              16 pt    Styles          Left        1.0     Tables
```

Dear Mr. Johnston:

WordPerfect for Windows includes many new a
features. A brief demonstration of this software
next Wednesday at 11 a.m. in the conference r

A lunch will follow the demonstration. We ho

Yours truly,

Mary Vickers

1 Select the text you want to change to a new case.

Note: To select text, refer to page 30.

66

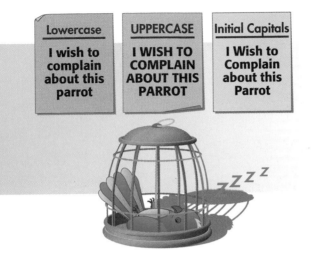

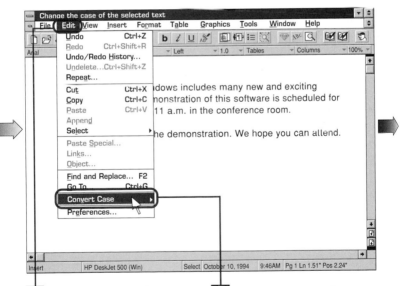

2 Move the mouse ☇ over **Edit** and then press the left button.

3 Move the mouse ☇ over **Convert Case** and then press the left button.

To continue, refer to the next page.

CHANGE THE CASE OF TEXT

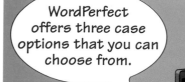

WordPerfect offers three case options that you can choose from.

CHANGE THE CASE OF TEXT (CONTINUED)

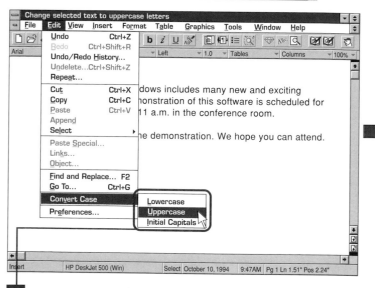

Change selected text to uppercase letters

File   Edit   View   Insert   Format   Table   Graphics   Tools   Window   Help

Arial

Undo	Ctrl+Z
Redo	Ctrl+Shift+R
Undo/Redo History...	
Undelete...Ctrl+Shift+Z	
Repeat...	
Cut	Ctrl+X
Copy	Ctrl+C
Paste	Ctrl+V
Append	
Select	▶
Paste Special...	
Links...	
Object...	
Find and Replace...	F2
Go To...	Ctrl+G
Convert Case	
Preferences...	

dows includes many new and exciting
nonstration of this software is scheduled for
11 a.m. in the conference room.

he demonstration. We hope you can attend.

Lowercase
Uppercase
Initial Capitals

Insert   HP DeskJet 500 (Win)   Select   October 10, 1994   9:47AM   Pg 1 Ln 1.51" Pos 2.24"

4 Move the mouse ⟋ over
the case you want to use
(example: **Uppercase**) and
then press the left button.

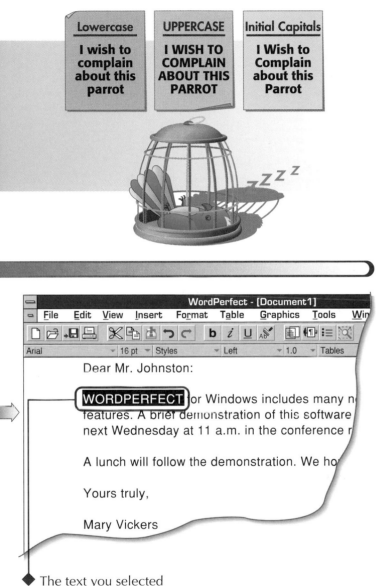

Lowercase	UPPERCASE	Initial Capitals
I wish to complain about this parrot	I WISH TO COMPLAIN ABOUT THIS PARROT	I Wish to Complain about this Parrot

WordPerfect - [Document1]

File Edit View Insert Format Table Graphics Tools Win

Arial   16 pt   Styles   Left   1.0   Tables

Dear Mr. Johnston:

WORDPERFECT or Windows includes many n
features. A brief demonstration of this software
next Wednesday at 11 a.m. in the conference r

A lunch will follow the demonstration. We ho

Yours truly,

Mary Vickers

◆ The text you selected
changes to the new case.

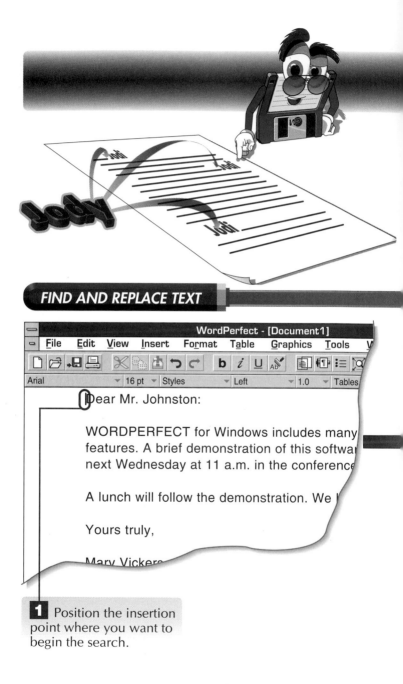

FIND AND REPLACE TEXT

WordPerfect - [Document1]

File Edit View Insert Format Table Graphics Tools

Arial   ▼ 16 pt ▼ Styles   ▼ Left   ▼ 1.0 ▼ Tables

Dear Mr. Johnston:

WORDPERFECT for Windows includes many
features. A brief demonstration of this softwa
next Wednesday at 11 a.m. in the conference

A lunch will follow the demonstration. We

Yours truly,

Mary Vickers

1 Position the insertion
point where you want to
begin the search.

70

You can use the Find and Replace feature to locate and replace every occurrence of a word or phrase in your document.

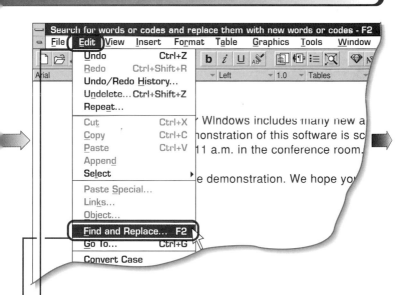

Search for words or codes and replace them with new words or codes - F2

File Edit View Insert Format Table Graphics Tools Window

Undo   Ctrl+Z
Redo   Ctrl+Shift+R
Undo/Redo History...
Undelete... Ctrl+Shift+Z
Repeat...

Cut   Ctrl+X
Copy   Ctrl+C
Paste   Ctrl+V
Append
Select

Paste Special...
Links...
Object...

Find and Replace... F2
Go To...   Ctrl+G
Convert Case

Arial   Left   1.0   Tables

r Windows includes many new a
onstration of this software is sc
11 a.m. in the conference room.

e demonstration. We hope you

2 Move the mouse Ⓚ over **Edit** and then press the left button.

3 Move the mouse ⓀＫ over **Find and Replace** and then press the left button.

◆ The **Find and Replace Text** dialog box appears.

To continue, refer to the next page.

71

4 Type the text you want to find (example: **Wednesday**).

5 Press **Tab** to move to the **Replace With:** box. Then type the text you want to replace the searched word (example: **Friday**).

The Find and Replace feature is ideal if you have frequently misspelled a name in your document.

WordPerfect - [Document1]

File   Edit   View   Insert   Format   Table   Graphics   Tools   Window   Help

Arial   16 pt   Styles   Left   1.0   Tables   Columns   100%

Dear Mr. Johnston:

WORDPERFECT for Windows includes many new and exciting features. A brief demonstration of this software is scheduled for next Wednesday at 11 a.m. in the conference room.

A lunch will follow the demonstration. We hope you can attend.

Yours truly,

Find and Replace Text

Type   Match   Replace   Direction   Action   Options

Find:

Wednesday   Find Next

Replace With: Replace

Friday   Replace All
                                              Close
                                              Help

Insert   HP DeskJet 500 (Win)   Select   October 10, 1994   9:55AM   Pg 1 Ln 2.01" Pos 2.65"

6 To start the search, move the mouse ⬚ over **Find Next** and then press the left button.

◆ WordPerfect highlights the first matching word it finds.

To continue, refer to the next page.

FIND AND REPLACE TEXT

You can close the Find and Replace Text dialog box at any time during the search.

WordPerfect - [Document1]

File   Edit   View   Insert   Format   Table   Graphics   Tools   Window   Help

Arial   16 pt   Styles   Left   1.0   Tables   Columns   100%

Dear Mr. Johnston:

WORDPERFECT for Windows includes many new and exciting features. A brief demonstration of this software is scheduled for next Wednesday at 11 a.m. in the conference room.

A lunch will follow the demonstration. We hope you can attend.

Yours truly,

Find and Replace Text

Type   Match   Replace   Direction   Action   Options

Find:
Wednesday

Replace With:
Friday

Find Next
Replace
Replace All
Close
Help

Insert   HP DeskJet 500 (Win)   Select   October 10, 1994   9:56AM   Pg 1 Ln 2.01" Pos 2.65"

7 To replace the word and search for the next occurrence, move the mouse ▷ over **Replace** and then press the left button.

Note: To ignore the word and search for the next occurrence, move the mouse ▷ over ***Find Next*** *and then press the left button.*

74

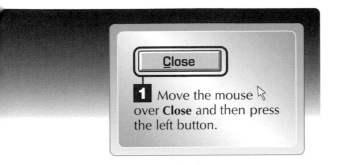

1 Move the mouse ⌖ over **Close** and then press the left button.

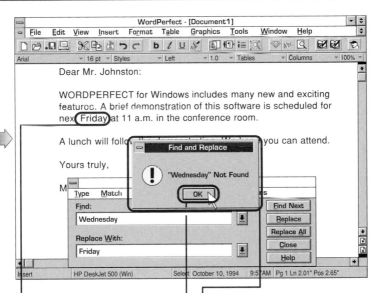

◆ WordPerfect replaces the word and searches for the next occurrence.

8 Repeat step **7** for each matching word that WordPerfect finds.

◆ This dialog box appears when WordPerfect cannot find any more occurrences of the word in your document.

9 To close the dialog box, move the mouse ⌖ over **OK** and then press the left button.

USING QUICKCORRECT

WordPerfect automatically corrects common spelling errors as you type. You can customize the QuickCorrect list to include words you often misspell.

ADD TEXT TO THE QUICKCORRECT LIST

nd spelling errors as you type - Ctrl+Shift+F1

w	Insert	Format	Table	Graphics	**Tools**	Window	Help

| | | b | *i* | U | A͟ᵦ | | |

| ᵖ | Styles | | Left | | 1.0 | |

Johnston:

ERFECT for Windows includes
A brief demonstration of this
y at 11 a.m. in the conferenc

follow the demonstration. \

Spell Check...	Ctrl+F1	
Thesaurus...	Alt+F1	
Grammatik...	Alt+Shift+F1	
QuickCorrect...	Ctrl+Shift+F1	
Language...		
Macro	▶	
Template Macro	▶	
Merge...	Shift+F9	
Sort...	Alt+F9	
Outline		
Hypertext		
List		
Index		
Cross-Reference		
Table of Contents		
Table of Authorities		

1 Move the mouse ⇧ over **Tools** and then press the left button.

2 Move the mouse ⇧ over **QuickCorrect** and then press the left button.

◆ The **QuickCorrect** dialog box appears.

76

Replace	With
artic	arctic
comittee	committee
Febuary	February
july	July
recieve	receive
teh	the
wierd	weird

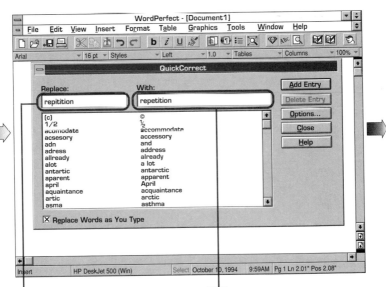

3 Type the text you want WordPerfect to automatically correct every time you type it in a document (example: **repitition**).

4 Press **Tab** to move to the **With:** box. Then type the correct spelling of the word (example: **repetition**).

To continue, refer to the next page.

USING QUICKCORRECT

After you add text to the QuickCorrect list, WordPerfect will automatically change the text every time you type it in a document.

ADD TEXT TO THE QUICKCORRECT LIST (CONTINUED)

```
                        WordPerfect - [Document1]
 File   Edit   View   Insert   Format   Table   Graphics   Tools   Window   Help
Arial            ▾ 16 pt ▾ Styles        ▾ Left      ▾ 1.0  ▾ Tables       ▾ Columns      ▾ 100% ▾
                              QuickCorrect

 Replace:                  With:                              Add Entry
 repitition                repetition                         Delete Entry

 (c)                       ©                          ↑       Options...
 1/2                       ½
 acomodate                 accommodate                        Close
 acsesory                  accessory
 adn                       and                                Help
 adress                    address
 allready                  already
 alot                      a lot
 antartic                  antarctic
 aparent                   apparent
 april                     April
 aquaintance               acquaintance
 artic                     arctic
 asma                      asthma                     ↓

 ☒ Replace Words as You Type

Insert        HP DeskJet 500 (Win)     Select  October 10, 1994    10:00AM  Pg 1 Ln 2.01" Pos 2.08"
```

5 Move the mouse ⟍ over **Add Entry** and then press the left button.

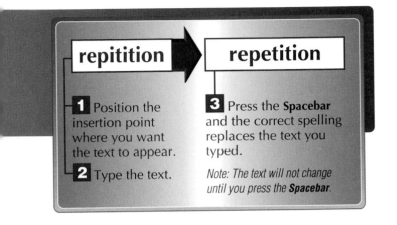

repitition ➜ **repetition**

1 Position the insertion point where you want the text to appear.

2 Type the text.

3 Press the **Spacebar** and the correct spelling replaces the text you typed.

*Note: The text will not change until you press the **Spacebar**.*

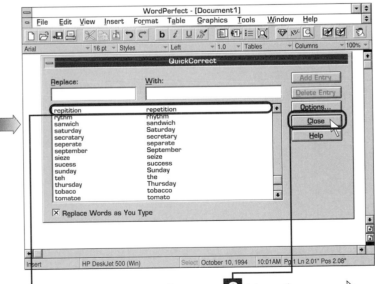

◆ The entry appears in the QuickCorrect list.

6 Move the mouse over **Close** and then press the left button.

CHECK SPELLING

You can use the Spelling feature to find and correct spelling errors in your document.

CHECK SPELLING

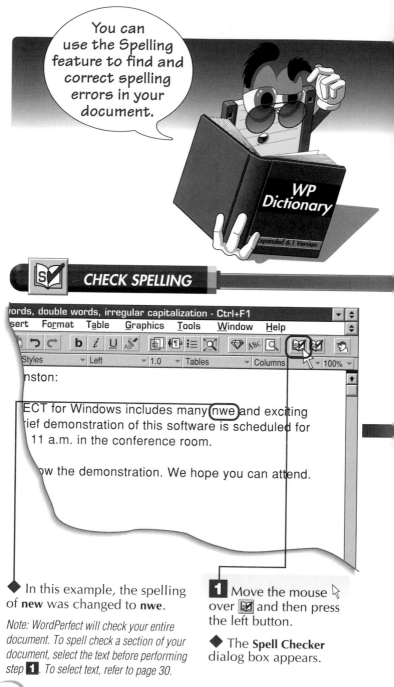

vords, double words, irregular capitalization - Ctrl+F1

sert   Format   Table   Graphics   Tools   Window   Help

Styles   Left   1.0   Tables   Columns   100%

nston:

ECT for Windows includes many (nwe) and exciting
rief demonstration of this software is scheduled for
11 a.m. in the conference room.

w the demonstration. We hope you can attend.

◆ In this example, the spelling of **new** was changed to **nwe**.

Note: WordPerfect will check your entire document. To spell check a section of your document, select the text before performing step **1**. *To select text, refer to page 30.*

1 Move the mouse ⬚ over 🔲 and then press the left button.

◆ The **Spell Checker** dialog box appears.

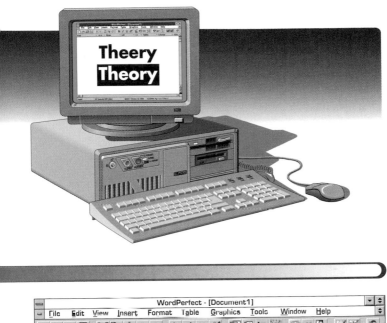

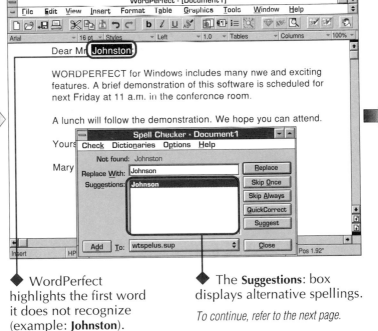

◆ WordPerfect highlights the first word it does not recognize (example: **Johnston**).

◆ The **Suggestions**: box displays alternative spellings.

To continue, refer to the next page.

CHECK SPELLING

WordPerfect compares every word in your document to words in its dictionary. If a word does not exist in the dictionary, WordPerfect considers it misspelled.

WP Dictionary

Expanded 6.1 Version

CHECK SPELLING (CONTINUED)

WordPerfect - [Document1]

File Edit View Insert Format Table Graphics Tools Window Help

Arial   16 pt   Styles   Left   1.0   Tables   Columns   100%

Dear Mr. Johnston:

WORDPERFECT for Windows includes many nwe and exciting features. A brief demonstration of this software is scheduled for next Friday at 11 a.m. in the conference room.

A lunch will follow the demonstration. We hope you can attend.

Yours

Mary

Spell Checker - Document1

Check Dictionaries Options Help

Not found: Johnston

Replace With: Johnson   Replace

Suggestions: Johnson   Skip Once

Skip Always

QuickCorrect

Suggest

Add To: wtspelus.sup   Close

Insert   HP   Pos 1.92"

Skip Misspelled Word

2 To skip the word and continue checking your document, move the mouse ⦃ over **Skip Once** and then press the left button.

*Note: To skip the word and all other occurrences of the word in your document, move the mouse ⦃ over **Skip Always** and then press the left button.*

82

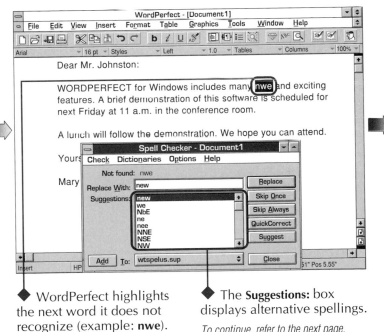

◆ WordPerfect highlights the next word it does not recognize (example: **nwe**).

◆ The **Suggestions:** box displays alternative spellings.

To continue, refer to the next page.

The Spelling feature will not find a correctly spelled word used in the wrong context.

CHECK SPELLING (CONTINUED)

Dear Mr. Johnston:

WORDPERFECT for Windows includes many nwe and exciting features. A brief demonstration of this software is scheduled for next Friday at 11 a.m. in the conference room.

A lunch will follow the demonstration. We hope you can attend.

Yours

Mary

Spell Checker - Document1

Check   Dictionaries   Options   Help

Not found: nwe

Replace With: new

Suggestions:
new
we
NbE
ne
nee
NNE
NSE
NW

Replace
Skip Once
Skip Always
QuickCorrect
Suggest

Add   To: wtspelus.sup

Close

Correct Misspelled Word

3 To select the correct spelling, move the mouse over the word (example: **new**) and then press the left button.

4 Move the mouse over **Replace** and then press the left button.

84

Example:

The girl is **sit** years old.

You must review your document carefully to find this type of error.

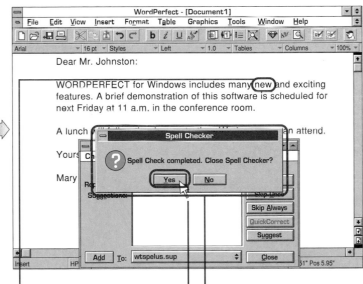

◆ WordPerfect corrects the word and continues checking your document.

5 Skip or correct spelling errors until WordPerfect finishes checking your document.

◆ This dialog box appears when the spell check is complete.

6 To close the **Spell Checker** dialog box, move the mouse ⤢ over **Yes** and then press the left button.

USING THE THESAURUS

The Thesaurus lets you replace a word in your document with one that is more suitable.

WP Thesaurus

New 6.1 Edition

USING THE THESAURUS

File Edit View Insert Format Table Graphics **Tools** Window Help

Arial   16 pt   Styles   Left   1.0

Tools menu
Spell Check...   Ctrl+F1
Thesaurus...   Alt+F1
Grammatik...   Alt+Shift+F1
QuickCorrect... Ctrl+Shift+F1
Language...
Macro ▶
Template Macro ▶
Merge...   Shift+F9
Sort...   Alt+F9
Outline
Hypertext
List
Index
Cross-Reference
Table of Contents
Table of Authorities
Generate...   Ctrl+F9

Dear Mr. Johnston:

WORDPERFECT for Windows includes
features. A brief demonstration of this
next Friday at 11 a.m. in the conferenc

A lunch will follow the demonstration. V

Yours truly,

Mary Vickers

Insert   HP DeskJet 500 (Win)   Select October 10, 1994   10:08AM Pg 1 Ln 1.76" Pos 2.32"

1 Position the insertion point anywhere in the word you want to look up (example: **brief**).

2 Move the mouse over **Tools** and then press the left button.

3 Move the mouse over **Thesaurus** and then press the left button.

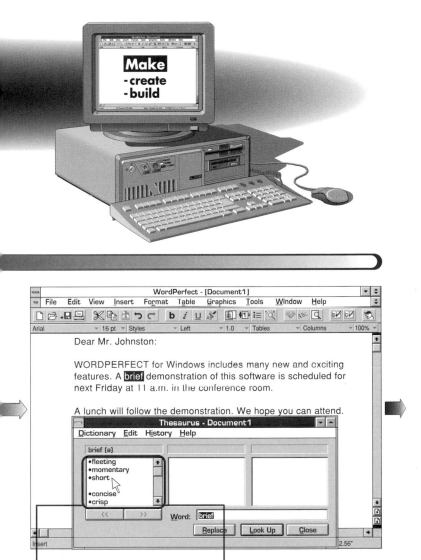

This area displays a list of alternative words.

Note: To view additional words in the list, use the scroll bar. For more information, refer to page 28.

4 To display terms related to a word in the list, move the mouse ⤢ over the word and then quickly press the left button twice.

To continue, refer to the next page.

USING THE THESAURUS

You can use the Thesaurus to add variety to your writing.
WP Thesaurus
New 6.1 Edition

USING THE THESAURUS (CONTINUED)

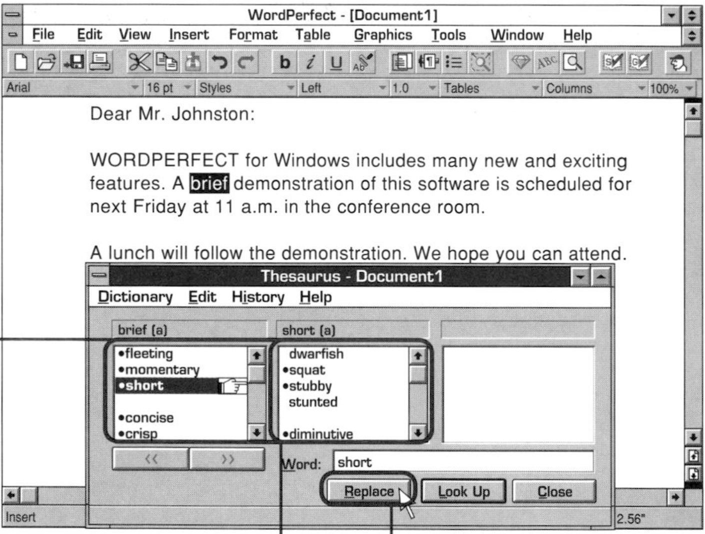
WordPerfect - [Document1]
File Edit View Insert Format Table Graphics Tools Window Help
Arial 16 pt Styles Left 1.0 Tables Columns 100%
Dear Mr. Johnston:
WORDPERFECT for Windows includes many new and exciting features. A brief demonstration of this software is scheduled for next Friday at 11 a.m. in the conference room.
A lunch will follow the demonstration. We hope you can attend.
Thesaurus - Document1
Dictionary Edit History Help
brief (a)
•fleeting
•momentary
•short
•concise
•crisp
short (a)
dwarfish
•squat
•stubby
stunted
•diminutive
Word: short
Replace
Look Up
Close
Insert
2.56"

◆ A list of alternative words appears.

5 To select the word you want to use, move the mouse over the word (example: **short**) and then press the left button.

6 Move the mouse over **Replace** and then press the left button.

*Note: To close the Thesaurus without changing the word in your document, move the mouse over **Close** and then press the left button.*

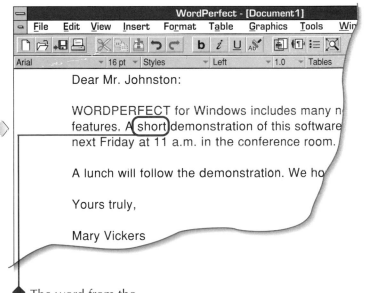

◆ The word from the Thesaurus replaces the word in your document.

CHECK GRAMMAR

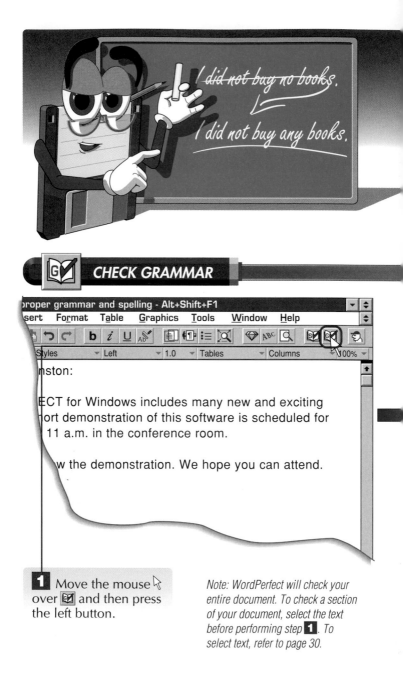

CHECK GRAMMAR

roper grammar and spelling - Alt+Shift+F1

sert   Fo_rmat   T_able   _Graphics   _Tools   _Window   _Help

Styles   Left   1.0   Tables   Columns   100%

nston:

ECT for Windows includes many new and exciting
ort demonstration of this software is scheduled for
11 a.m. in the conference room.

w the demonstration. We hope you can attend.

1 Move the mouse ⌖
over 📖 and then press
the left button.

*Note: WordPerfect will check your
entire document. To check a section
of your document, select the text
before performing step* **1**. *To
select text, refer to page 30.*

You can use
the Grammatik®
feature to find and
correct grammar and
spelling errors in your
document.

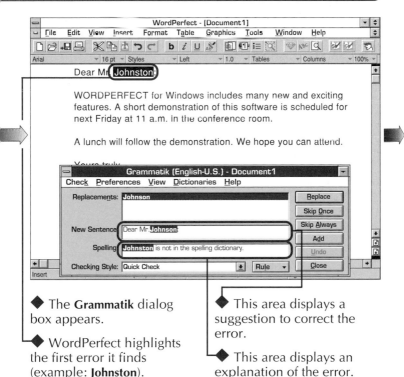

◆ The **Grammatik** dialog
box appears.

◆ WordPerfect highlights
the first error it finds
(example: **Johnston**).

◆ This area displays a
suggestion to correct the
error.

◆ This area displays an
explanation of the error.

To continue, refer to the next page.

CHECK GRAMMAR

CHECK GRAMMAR (CONTINUED)

Skip Grammatical Error

2 To skip the error and continue checking your document, move the mouse ⌖ over **Skip Once** and then press the left button.

*Note: To skip the error and all other occurrences of the error in your document, move the mouse ⌖ over **Skip Always** and then press the left button.*

When WordPerfect finds a grammatical error in your document, you can skip or correct the error.

WordPerfect - [Document1]

File   Edit   View   Insert   Format   Table   Graphics   Tools   Window   Help

Arial   16 pt   Styles   Left   1.0   Tables   Columns   100%

Dear Mr. Johnston:

WORDPERFECT for Windows includes many new and exciting features. A short demonstration of this software is scheduled for next Friday at **11** a.m. in the conference room.

A lunch will follow the demonstration. We hope you can attend.

Yours truly,

Grammatik (English-U.S.) - Document1

Check   Preferences   View   Dictionaries   Help

Replacements: **11:00**

New Sentence: A short demonstration of this software is scheduled for next Friday at **11:00** a.m. in the conference room.

Date and Time Format: Write out the complete time before **a.m.** ("11:00 a.m." instead of "11 a.m.").

Checking Style: Quick Check   Rule

Replace
Skip Once
Skip Always
Add
Undo
Close

Insert

Correct Grammatical Error

◆ WordPerfect highlights the next error it finds.

3 To correct the error, move the mouse ⊳ over **Replace** and then press the left button.

To continue, refer to the next page.

CHECK GRAMMAR

The Grammatik feature will improve the accuracy of your document.

CHECK GRAMMAR (CONTINUED)

WordPerfect - [Document1]

File   Edit   View   Insert   Format   Table   Graphics   Tools   Window   Help

Arial   16 pt   Styles   Left   1.0   Tables   Columns   100%

Dear Mr. Johnston:

WORDPERFECT for Windows includes many new and exciting features. A short demonstration of this software is scheduled for next Friday at 11:00 a.m. in the conference room.

A lunch will follow the demonstration. We hope you can attend.

Yours truly,

Grammatik (English-U.S.) - Document1

Check   Preferences   View   Dictionaries   Help

Replacements: 11:00

New Sentence: A short demonstration of this software is scheduled for next Friday at 11:00 a.m. in the conference room.

Date and Time Format: Write out the complete time before a.m. ("11:00 a.m." instead of "11 a.m.").

Checking Style: Quick Check   Rule

Replace
Skip Once
Skip Always
Add
Undo
Close

Insert

◆ WordPerfect corrects the error and continues checking your document.

4 Skip or correct grammatical errors until WordPerfect finishes checking your document.

94

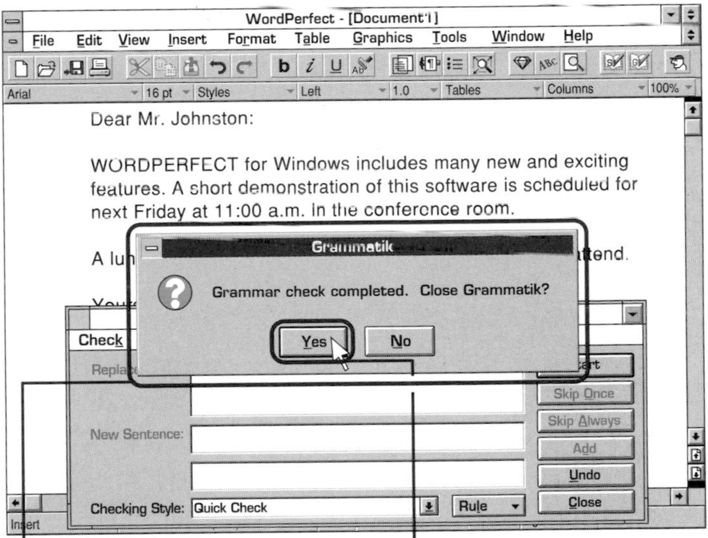

◆ This dialog box appears when the grammar check is complete.

5 To close the **Grammatik** dialog box, move the mouse over **Yes** and then press the left button.

SAVE A NEW DOCUMENT

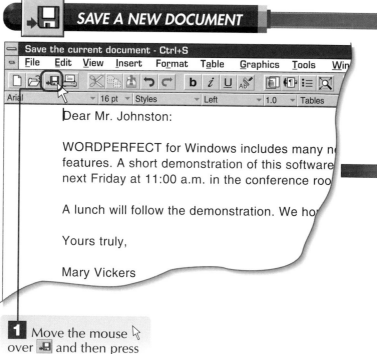

SAVE A NEW DOCUMENT

Save the current document - Ctrl+S

File   Edit   View   Insert   Format   Table   Graphics   Tools   Win

Arial   16 pt Styles   Left   1.0 Tables

Dear Mr. Johnston:

WORDPERFECT for Windows includes many n
features. A short demonstration of this software
next Friday at 11:00 a.m. in the conference roo

A lunch will follow the demonstration. We ho

Yours truly,

Mary Vickers

1 Move the mouse ⌖ over 🔲 and then press the left button.

You should save your document to store it for future use. This enables you to later retrieve the document for reviewing or editing purposes.

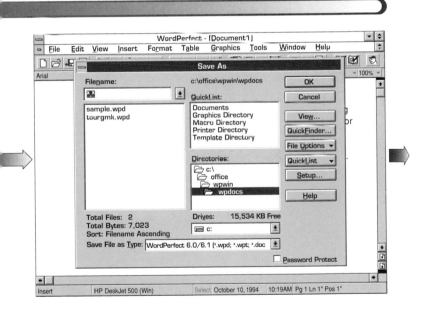

◆ The **Save As** dialog box appears.

*Note: If you previously saved your document, the **Save As** dialog box will **not** appear since you have already named the document.*

To continue, refer to the next page.

SAVE A NEW DOCUMENT

A filename consists of a name and an extension.

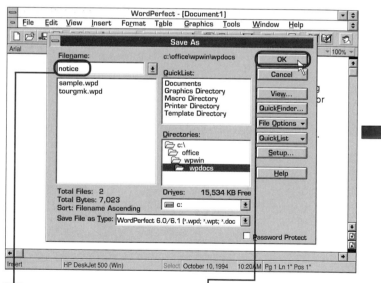

2 Type a name for your document (example: **notice**).

*Note: To make it easier to find your document later on, do not type an extension. WordPerfect will automatically add the **wpd** extension to the filename.*

3 Move the mouse ⩗ over **OK** and then press the left button.

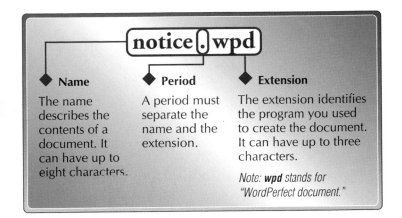

Name

The name describes the contents of a document. It can have up to eight characters.

Period

A period must separate the name and the extension.

Extension

The extension identifies the program you used to create the document. It can have up to three characters.

*Note: **wpd** stands for "WordPerfect document."*

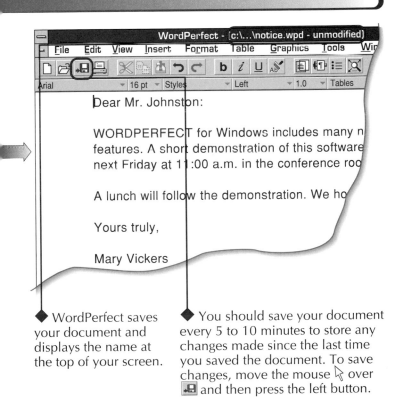

◆ WordPerfect saves your document and displays the name at the top of your screen.

◆ You should save your document every 5 to 10 minutes to store any changes made since the last time you saved the document. To save changes, move the mouse ⟲ over 🔲 and then press the left button.

SAVE A DOCUMENT TO A DISKETTE

SAVE A DOCUMENT TO A DISKETTE

MicroFLOPPY
Double Sided

Today's Disk

1 Insert a diskette into a floppy drive (example: **a:**).

If you want to give your colleagues a copy of a document, you can save the document to a diskette. They can then review the document on their own computers.

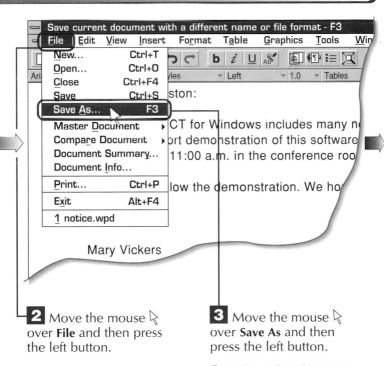

2 Move the mouse ⟨ over **File** and then press the left button.

3 Move the mouse ⟨ over **Save As** and then press the left button.

To continue, refer to the next page.

SAVE A DOCUMENT TO A DISKETTE

Most computers have one hard drive and one or two floppy drives to store information.

SAVE A DOCUMENT TO A DISKETTE (CONTINUED)

WordPerfect - [c:\...\notice.wpd - unmodified]

File   Edit   View   Insert   Format   Table   Graphics   Tools   Window   Help

Arial

Save As

Filename: c:\office\wpwin\wpdocs

notice.wpd

notice.wpd
sample.wpd
tourgmk.wpd

QuickList:

Documents
Graphics Directory
Macro Directory
Printer Directory
Template Directory

Directories:

c:\
  office
    wpwin
      wpdocs

OK
Cancel
View...
QuickFinder...
File Options ▼
QuickList ▼
Setup...
Help

Total Files: 3
Total Bytes: 9,949
Sort: Filename Ascending

Drives: 15,534 KB Free

c:

Save File as Type: WordPerfect 6.0/6.1 [*.wpd; *.wpt; *.doc ▼

☐ Password Protect

Insert   HP DeskJet 500 (Win)   Select October 10, 1994   10:23AM Pg 1 Ln 1" Pos 1"

◆ The **Save As** dialog box appears.

4 The **Filename:** box displays the current filename. To save your document with a different name, type a new name.

◆ The **Drives:** box displays the current drive (example: **c:**).

5 To save the document to a diskette, move the mouse ⌖ over ⬇ in the **Drives:** box and then press the left button.

Hard drive (c:)

◆ The hard drive magnetically stores information inside your computer.

*Note: Your computer may be set up to have additional hard drives (example: drive **d**).*

Floppy drives (a: and b:)

◆ A floppy drive stores information on removable diskettes (or floppy disks). A diskette operates slower and stores less data than a hard drive.

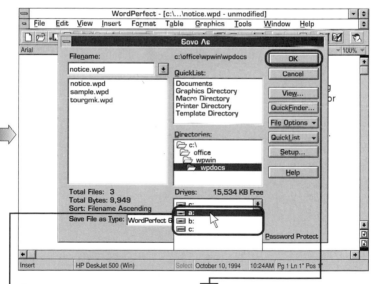

◆ A list of the available drives for the computer appears.

6 Move the mouse ⬚ over the drive you want to use (example: **a:**) and then press the left button.

7 To save your document, move the mouse ⬚ over **OK** and then press the left button.

EXIT WORDPERFECT

When you finish using WordPerfect, you can exit the program to return to the Windows Program Manager.

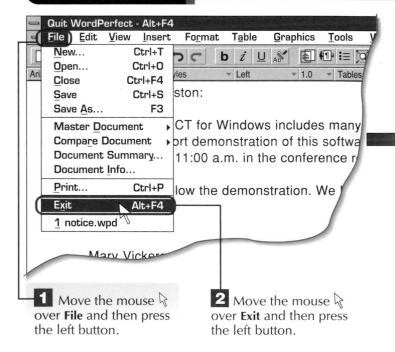

Quit WordPerfect - Alt+F4

File   Edit   View   Insert   Format   Table   Graphics   Tools

New...	Ctrl+T
Open...	Ctrl+O
Close	Ctrl+F4
Save	Ctrl+S
Save As...	F3

Master Document
Compare Document
Document Summary...
Document Info...

Print...   Ctrl+P

Exit   Alt+F4

1 notice.wpd

...ston:

...CT for Windows includes many
...ort demonstration of this softwa
...11:00 a.m. in the conference r

...low the demonstration. We

Mary Vicker

1 Move the mouse ⟍ over **File** and then press the left button.

2 Move the mouse ⟍ over **Exit** and then press the left button.

104

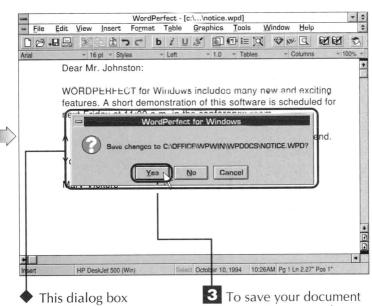

◆ This dialog box appears if you have not saved changes made to your document.

Note: For more information on saving a document, refer to page 96.

3 To save your document before exiting, move the mouse ⌖ over **Yes** and then press the left button.

*Note: To exit without saving your document, move the mouse ⌖ over **No** and then press the left button.*

OPEN A DOCUMENT

OPEN A DOCUMENT

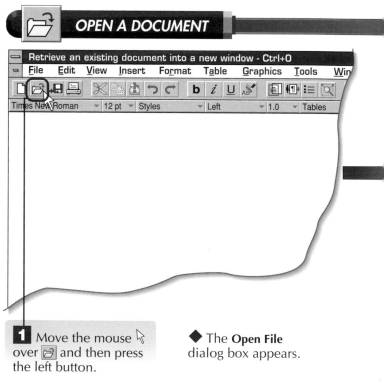

Retrieve an existing document into a new window - Ctrl+O

| File | Edit | View | Insert | Format | Table | Graphics | Tools | Win |

Times New Roman ▼ 12 pt ▼ Styles ▼ Left ▼ 1.0 ▼ Tables

1 Move the mouse ▯ over 🖿 and then press the left button.

◆ The **Open File** dialog box appears.

You can open
a saved document
and display it on
your screen.

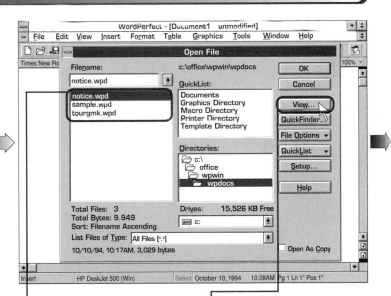

2 Move the mouse ▷ over the name of the document you want to open (example: **notice.wpd**) and then press the left button.

3 To preview the document, move the mouse ▷ over **View** and then press the left button.

To continue, refer to the next page.

107

OPEN A DOCUMENT

OPEN A DOCUMENT (CONTINUED)

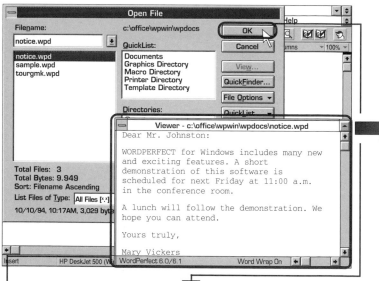

◆ The contents of the document appear.

Note: To view the contents of another document, repeat step **2** *on page 107.*

4 To open this document, move the mouse ⊳ over **OK** and then press the left button.

108

After opening a document, you can review and edit your work.

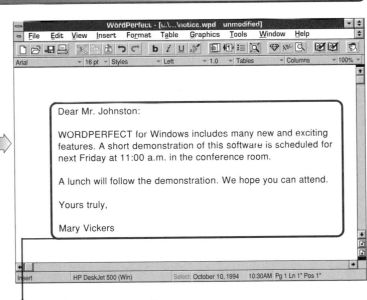

◆ WordPerfect opens the
document and displays it
on your screen. You can now
make changes to the document.

OPEN A DOCUMENT

QUICKLY OPEN A DOCUMENT

Open File - c:\office\wpwin\wpdocs\notice.wpd

| File | Edit | View | Insert | Format | Table | Graphics | Tools | W |

New...	Ctrl+T	
Open...	Ctrl+O	
Close	Ctrl+F4	
Save	Ctrl+S	
Save **A**s...	F3	

Master **D**ocument ▶
Compare Document ▶
Document Summary...
Document **I**nfo...

Print...	Ctrl+P
E**x**it	Alt+F4

1 notice.wpd

1 Move the mouse ⏳ over **File** and then press the left button.

2 Move the mouse ⏳ over the name of the document you want to open (example: **notice.wpd**) and then press the left button.

Note: In this example, only one document has been opened.

110

The File menu displays the names of the last four documents you opened. You can easily display one of these documents on your screen.

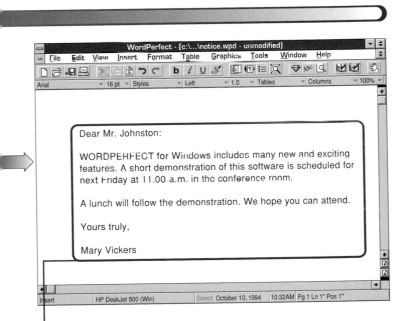

◆ WordPerfect opens the document and displays it on your screen. You can now make changes to the document.

DISPLAY DOCUMENT INFORMATION

Document Information

234	Character Count
44	Word Count
11	Line Count
9	Sentence Count
	Paragraph Count
1	Page Count
5	Average Word Length
4	Average Words Per Sentence
13	Maximum Words Per Sentence

OK

DISPLAY DOCUMENT INFORMATION

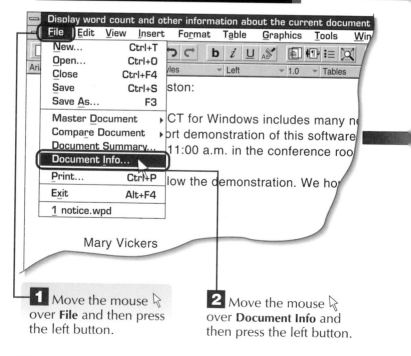

Display word count and other information about the current document

File Edit View Insert Format Table Graphics Tools Win

New...   Ctrl+T
Open...   Ctrl+O
Close   Ctrl+F4
Save   Ctrl+S
Save As...   F3

Master Document   ▶
Compare Document   ▶
Document Summary...
Document Info...

Print...   Ctrl+P
Exit   Alt+F4

1 notice.wpd

Ari   yles   Left   1.0   Tables

ston:

CT for Windows includes many n
ort demonstration of this software
11:00 a.m. in the conference roo

low the demonstration. We ho

Mary Vickers

1 Move the mouse ⋏ over **File** and then press the left button.

2 Move the mouse ⋏ over **Document Info** and then press the left button.

112

Before printing a document, you can display the word count, number of pages and other information about the document.

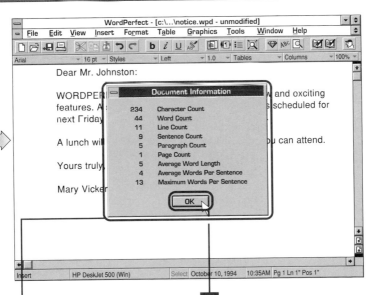

◆ This dialog box appears displaying information about your document.

3 To close the dialog box, move the mouse ▷ over **OK** and then press the left button.

113

PRINT A DOCUMENT

Print a document - Ctrl+P

| File | Edit | View | Insert | Format | Table | Graphics | Tools | Win |

Arial ▼ 16 pt ▼ Styles ▼ Left ▼ 1.0 ▼ Tables

Dear Mr. Johnston:

WORDPERFECT for Windows includes many n
features. A short demonstration of this software
next Friday at 11:00 a.m. in the conference roo

A lunch will follow the demonstration. We ho

Yours truly,

Mary Vickers

1 To print your entire document, move the mouse over ▣ and then press the left button.

◆ The **Print** dialog box appears.

Before printing
your document, make
sure your printer is
on and contains
paper.

WordPerfect - [c:\...\notice.wpd - unmodified]

File   Edit   View   Insert   Format   Table   Graphics   Tools   Window   Help

Arial   16 pt   Styles   Left   1.0   Tables   Columns   100%

Print

Current Printer
HP DeskJet 500 on LPT1: - WIN   Select...

Print Selection   Copies
⦿ Full Document   Number of Copies: 1
○ Current Page
○ Multiple Pages   Generated By: WordPerfect
○ Selected Text
○ Document Summary   Document Settings
○ Document on Disk   Print Quality: High
                             Print Color: Black
                             ☐ Do Not Print Graphics

Print
Close
Initialize
Options...
Control...
Help

Insert   HP DeskJet 500 (Win)   Select October 10, 1994   10:37AM Pg 1 Ln 1" Pos 1"

2 Move the mouse ▷
over **Full Document** and
then press the left button.

3 Move the mouse ▷
over **Print** and then press
the left button.

PRINT AN ENVELOPE

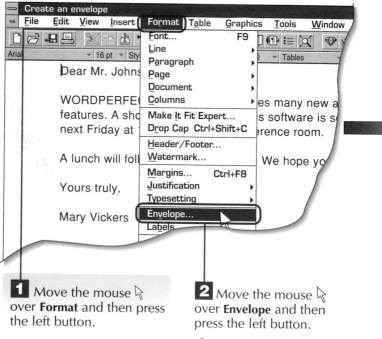

1 Move the mouse ⍺ over **Format** and then press the left button.

2 Move the mouse ⍺ over **Envelope** and then press the left button.

◆ The **Envelope** dialog box appears.

You can use the Envelope feature to create and then print an envelope.

WordPerfect - [c:\...\notice.wpd - unmodified]

File   Edit   View   Insert   Format   Table   Graphics   Tools   Window   Help

Envelope

Arial

Return Addresses

Mary Vickers
27 Willow Avenue
Los Angeles, CA 90032

<New Address>

Add   Delete   Font...

☒ Print Return Address

Mailing Addresses

<New Address>

Add   Delete   Font...

Mary Vickers
27 Willow Avenue
Los Angeles, CA 90032

WD

Envelopes

Envelope Definitions:

Envelope #10 Landscape

Size: 4.13"X 9.5"

Create New Definition...

Print Envelope   Append to Doc   Options...   Close   Help

Insert   HP DeskJet 500 (Win)   Select October 10, 1994   10:39AM Pg 1 Ln 1" Pos 1"

3 To enter a return address, move the mouse I over this area and then press the left button.

4 Type the return address. Press **Enter** after you type each line of text.

◆ If you do not want to print a return address, leave this area blank.

To continue, refer to the next page.

PRINT AN ENVELOPE (CONTINUED)

5 To enter the mailing address, move the mouse I over this area and then press the left button.

Note: A mailing address automatically appears in this area if WordPerfect finds one in the current document.

6 Type the mailing address. Press **Enter** after you type each line of text.

The Envelope
dialog box shows
you what your envelope
will look like when
printed.

WordPerfect - [c:\...\notice.wpd - unmodified]

File   Edit   View   Insert   Format   Table   Graphics   Tools   Window   Help

Envelope

Arial

Return Addresses

Mary Vickers
27 Willow Avenue
Los Angeles, CA 90032

<New Address>

Add   Delete   Font...

☒ Print Return Address

Mailing Addresses

Mr Johnston
248 Maple Crescent
Fullerton, CA 92740

<New Address>

Add   Delete   Font...

Mary Vickers
27 Willow Avenue
Los Angeles, CA 90032

Mr Johnston
248 Maple Crescent
Fullerton, CA 92740

Envelopes

Envelope Definitions:

Envelope #10 Landscape

Size: 4.13"X 9.5"

Create New Definition...

Print Envelope   Append to Doc   Options...   Close   Help

Insert   HP DeskJet 500 (Win)   Select   October 10, 1994   10:41AM   Pg 1 Ln 1" Pos 1"

◆ This area shows what
your envelope will look
like when printed.

7 To print the envelope,
move the mouse ⩗ over
Print Envelope and then
press the left button.

CHANGE MODES

WordPerfect offers three different ways to display your document.

DRAFT MODE

◆ The **Draft** mode simplifies the page so you can quickly type and edit your document.

◆ This mode does not display top or bottom margins, headers, footers or page numbers.

TWO PAGE MODE

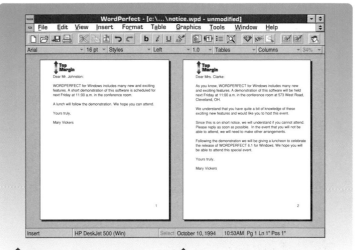

◆ The **Two Page** mode displays two consecutive pages side by side.

◆ This mode displays top and bottom margins, headers, footers and page numbers.

PAGE MODE

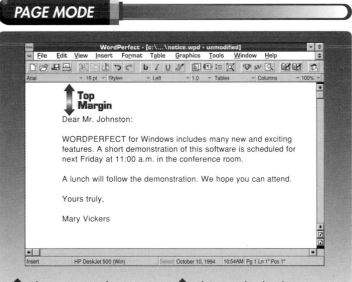

◆ The **Page** mode displays your document exactly the way it will appear on a printed page.

◆ This mode displays top and bottom margins, headers, footers and page numbers.

CHANGE MODES

You can easily display your document in a different mode to better suit your needs.

CHANGE THE DOCUMENT MODE

Display the document with headers and footers - Alt+F5

| File | Edit | View | Insert | Format | Table | Graphics | Tools |

√ Draft   Ctrl+F5
Page   Alt+F5
Two Page

Zoom...

√ Toolbar
√ Power Bar
Ruler Bar   Alt+Shift+F3
√ Status Bar
Hide Bars   Alt+Shift+F5

√ Graphics
Table Gridlines
Hidden Text
Show ¶   Ctrl+Shift+F3
Reveal Codes

1 Move the mouse ⓘ over **View** and then press the left button.

2 Move the mouse ⓘ over the mode you want to use (example: **Page**) and then press the left button.

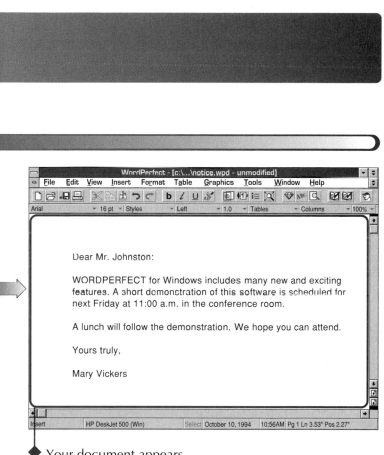

◆ Your document appears
in the new mode.

ZOOM IN OR OUT

ZOOM IN OR OUT

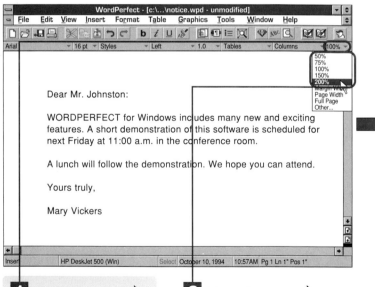

WordPerfect - [c:\...\notice.wpd - unmodified]

File   Edit   View   Insert   Format   Table   Graphics   Tools   Window   Help

Arial   16 pt   Styles   Left   1.0   Tables   Columns   100%

50%
75%
100%
150%
200%
Margin Width
Page Width
Full Page
Other...

Dear Mr. Johnston:

WORDPERFECT for Windows includes many new and exciting features. A short demonstration of this software is scheduled for next Friday at 11:00 a.m. in the conference room.

A lunch will follow the demonstration. We hope you can attend.

Yours truly,

Mary Vickers

Insert   HP DeskJet 500 (Win)   Select   October 10, 1994   10:57AM Pg 1 Ln 1" Pos 1"

1 Move the mouse ⬚ over 100% ▼ and then press the left button.

Note: You cannot use the Zoom feature if your document is displayed in the Two Page mode. To change modes, refer to page 122.

2 Move the mouse ⬚ over the zoom setting you want to use (example: **200%**) and then press the left button.

124

WordPerfect lets you enlarge or reduce the display of text on your screen.

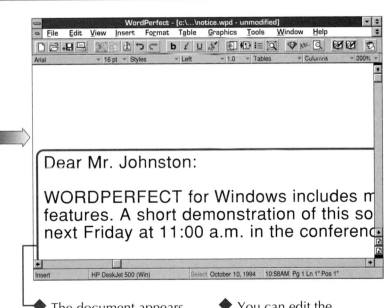

♦ The document appears in the new zoom setting.

Note: In this example, the document is displayed in the Page mode. If your document is displayed in the Draft mode, the results of using the Zoom feature will look different.

♦ You can edit the document as usual.

*Note: To return to the original zoom setting, repeat steps **1** and **2**, selecting **100%** in step **2**.*

SELECT A TOOLBAR

SELECT A TOOLBAR

WordPerfect - [c:\...\notice.wpd - unmodified]

File Edit View Insert Format Table Graphics Tools Window Help

√6.1 WordPerfect
Design Tools
Equation Editor
Font
Format
Generate
Graphics
Legal
Macro Tools
Page
Tables
Utilities
Workgroup

Edit...
Preferences...
Hide Toolbar

Arial   Left   1.0   Tables   Columns   100%

D

W   r Windows includes many new and exciting
fe   monstration of this software is scheduled for
n   a.m. in the conference room.

A   e demonstration. We hope you can attend.

Y

M

Insert   HP DeskJet 500 (Win)   Select October 10, 1994   10:59AM Pg 1 Ln 1" Pos 1"

◆ The **6.1 WordPerfect** Toolbar appears when you first start WordPerfect.

1 To display a different Toolbar, move the mouse ⬚ anywhere over the Toolbar and then press the **right** button.

◆ A list of the available Toolbars appears.

2 Move the mouse ⬚ over the name of the Toolbar you want to display (example: **Font**) and then press the left button.

Each Toolbar contains buttons to help you quickly perform specific tasks. You can display one of these Toolbars at any time.

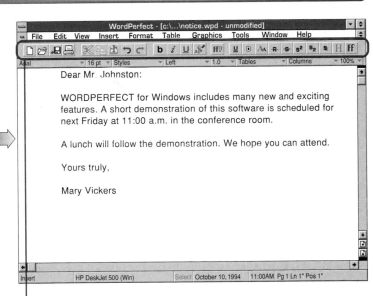

◆ The Toolbar you selected appears.

Note: To return to the original Toolbar, repeat steps **1** *and* **2**, *selecting* **6.1 WordPerfect** *in step* **2**.

CREATE A NEW DOCUMENT

You can create a document to start a new letter, report or memo.

CREATE A NEW DOCUMENT

Create a blank document in a new window - Ctrl+N

File Edit View Insert Format Table Graphics Tools

Arial   16 pt   Styles   Left   1.0   Tables

Dear Mr. Johnston:

WORDPERFECT for Windows includes many features. A short demonstration of this softwa next Friday at 11:00 a.m. in the conference r

A lunch will follow the demonstration. We

Yours truly,

Mary Vickers

1 Move the mouse ⌖ over ▯ and then press the left button.

◆ A new document appears.

Note: The previous document is now hidden behind the new document.

SWITCH BETWEEN DOCUMENTS

WordPerfect lets you have nine documents open at once. You can easily switch between all of these open documents.

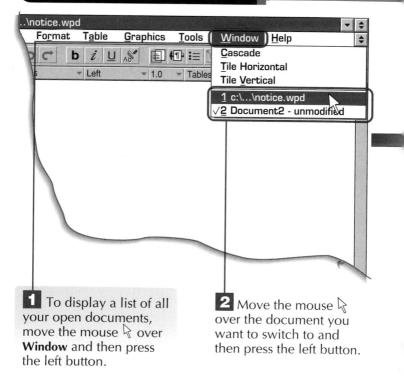

..\notice.wpd

Format   Table   Graphics   Tools   Window   Help

b *i* U

Left   1.0   Tables

Cascade
Tile Horizontal
Tile Vertical

1 c:\...\notice.wpd
√2 Document2 - unmodified

1 To display a list of all your open documents, move the mouse ⌖ over **Window** and then press the left button.

2 Move the mouse ⌖ over the document you want to switch to and then press the left button.

130

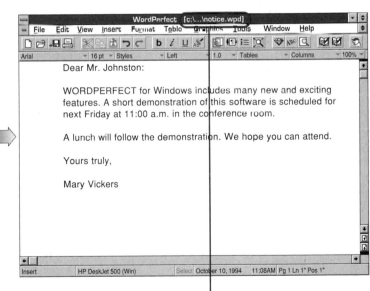

◆ The document appears.

◆ WordPerfect displays the name of the document at the top of your screen.

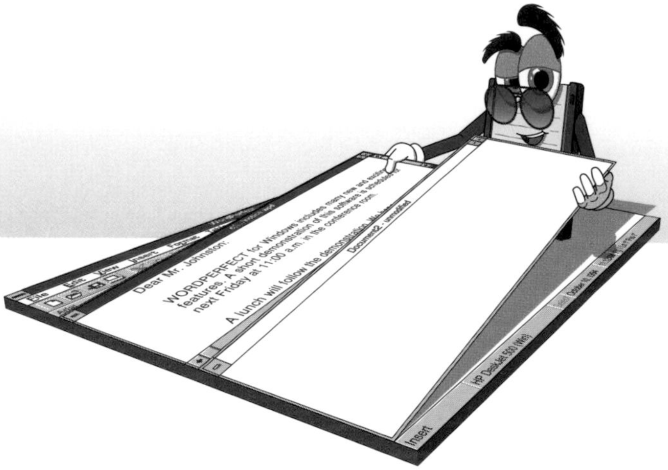

TILE OPEN DOCUMENTS

TILE OPEN DOCUMENTS

ws horizontally so you can see them all
Format Table Graphics Tools Window Help
Left 1.0 Tables
Cascade
Tile Horizontal
Tile Vertical
✓1 c:\...\notice.wpd
2 Document2 - unmodified
on:
T for Windows includes many new and exciting
t demonstration of this software is scheduled for
:00 a.m. in the conference room.
he demonstration. We hope you can attend.

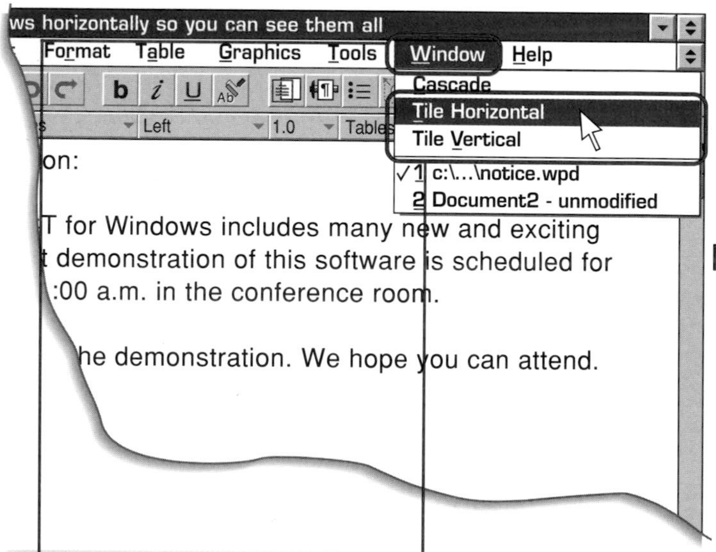

1 To tile all of your open documents, move the mouse over **Window** and then press the left button.

2 Move the mouse over the Tile option you want to use and then press the left button.

You can use the Tile command to view the contents of all of your open documents.

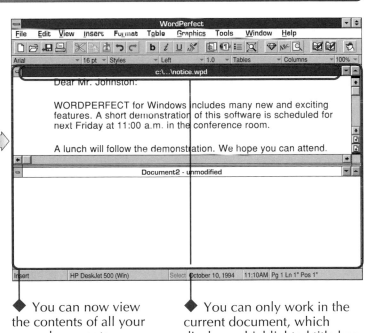

◆ You can now view the contents of all your open documents.

◆ You can only work in the current document, which displays a highlighted title bar.

Note: To make another document current, move the mouse ⟨⟩ anywhere over the document and then press the left button.

Copying or moving text between documents saves you time when you are working in one document and want to use text from another.

COPY OR MOVE TEXT BETWEEN DOCUMENTS

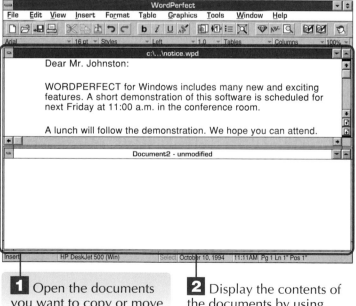

1 Open the documents you want to copy or move text between.

Note: To open a saved document, refer to page 106. To create a new document, refer to page 128.

2 Display the contents of the documents by using the Tile feature.

Note: To tile open documents, refer to page 132.

134

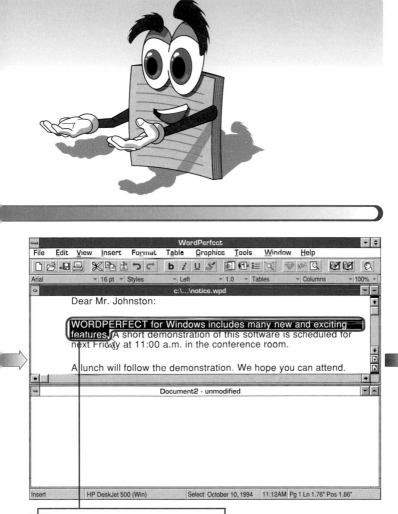

3 Select the text you want to copy or move to another document.

Note: To select text, refer to page 30.

4 Move the mouse I over the text you selected and I changes to ⬚.

To continue, refer to the next page.

COPY OR MOVE TEXT BETWEEN DOCUMENTS

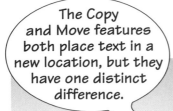

The Copy and Move features both place text in a new location, but they have one distinct difference.

COPY OR MOVE TEXT (CONTINUED)

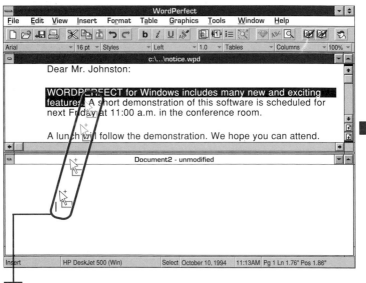

5 To copy the text, press and hold down **Ctrl** and then press and hold down the left button as you drag the mouse to where you want to place the text.

◆ To move the text, press and hold down the left button as you drag the mouse to where you want to place the text.

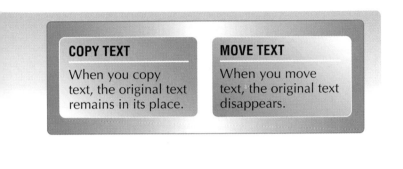

COPY TEXT

When you copy text, the original text remains in its place.

MOVE TEXT

When you move text, the original text disappears.

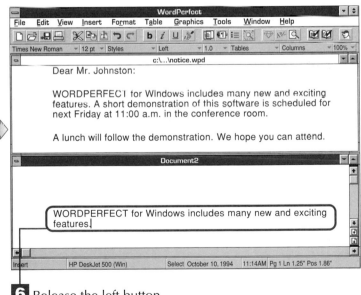

6 Release the left button (and **Ctrl**) and the text appears in the new location.

CLOSE A DOCUMENT

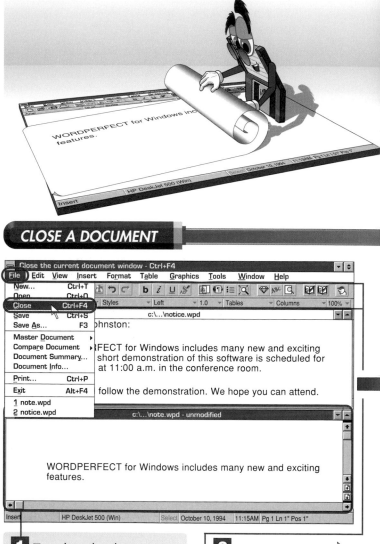

CLOSE A DOCUMENT

1 To select the document you want to close, move the mouse I over the document and then press the left button.

2 To save the document before closing, refer to page 96.

3 Move the mouse ⌖ over **File** and then press the left button.

4 Move the mouse ⌖ over **Close** and then press the left button.

138

> When you
> finish working with
> a document, you can
> close it to remove the
> document from
> your screen.

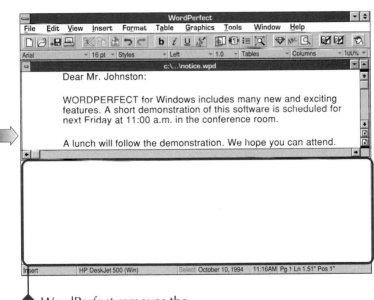

◆ WordPerfect removes the
document from your screen.

MAXIMIZE A DOCUMENT

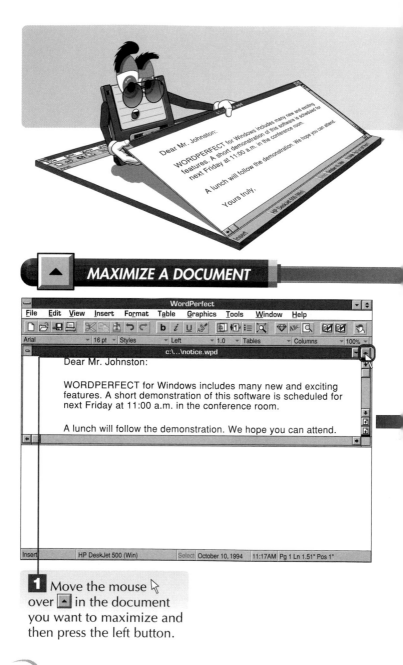

MAXIMIZE A DOCUMENT

1 Move the mouse ⌖ over ▲ in the document you want to maximize and then press the left button.

You can enlarge a document to fill your screen. This lets you view more of its contents.

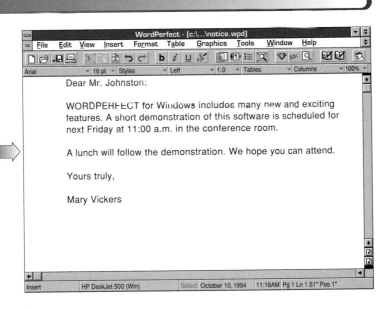

◆ The document enlarges to fill your screen.

BOLD, ITALIC AND UNDERLINE

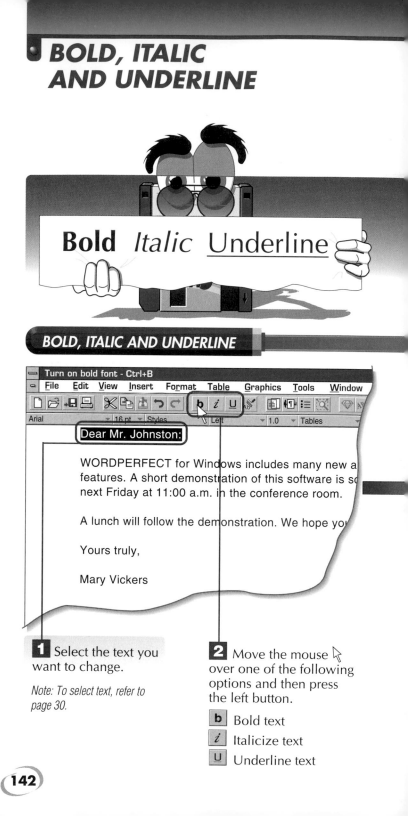

Bold *Italic* <u>Underline</u>

BOLD, ITALIC AND UNDERLINE

Turn on bold font - Ctrl+B

File   Edit   View   Insert   Format   Table   Graphics   Tools   Window

Arial   16 pt   Styles   Left   1.0   Tables

Dear Mr. Johnston:

WORDPERFECT for Windows includes many new a
features. A short demonstration of this software is so
next Friday at 11:00 a.m. in the conference room.

A lunch will follow the demonstration. We hope yo

Yours truly,

Mary Vickers

1 Select the text you want to change.

Note: To select text, refer to page 30.

2 Move the mouse over one of the following options and then press the left button.

b Bold text

i Italicize text

<u>U</u> Underline text

142

You can use the Bold, Italic and Underline features to emphasize important information.

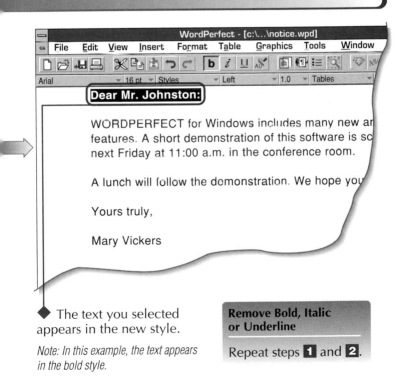

◆ The text you selected appears in the new style.

Note: In this example, the text appears in the bold style.

Remove Bold, Italic or Underline

Repeat steps **1** and **2**.

CHANGE FONT SIZE

6 point

12 point

14 point

18 point

24 point

WordPerfect measures the size of text in points. There are approximately 72 points per inch.

CHANGE FONT SIZE

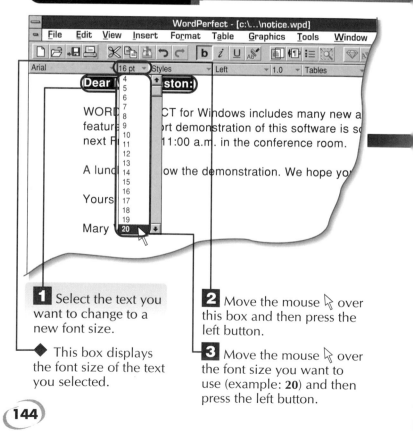

1 Select the text you want to change to a new font size.

◆ This box displays the font size of the text you selected.

2 Move the mouse ℝ over this box and then press the left button.

3 Move the mouse ℝ over the font size you want to use (example: **20**) and then press the left button.

144

You can increase
or decrease the size
of text in your document.
Increasing the size of text
can make your document
easier to read.

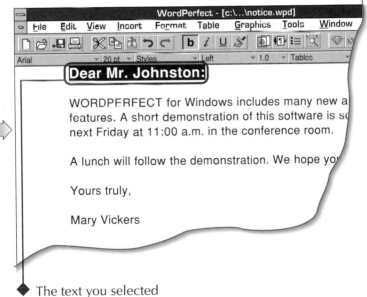

The text you selected
changes to the new font size.

CHANGE FONT FACE

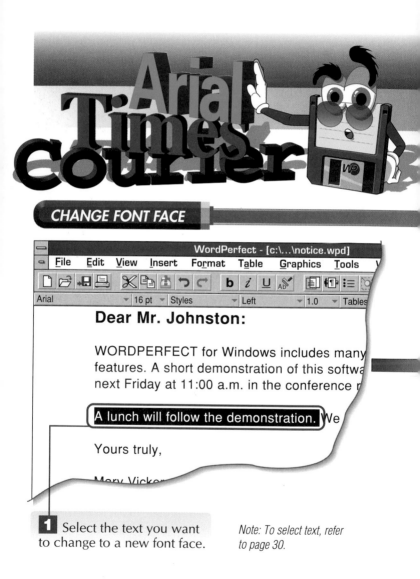

CHANGE FONT FACE

1 Select the text you want to change to a new font face.

Note: To select text, refer to page 30.

146

You can change the design of text to give your document a different look.

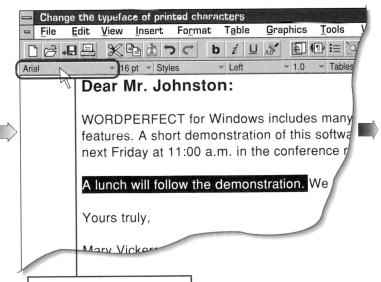

◆ This box displays the font face of the text you selected.

2 To display a list of the available font faces, move the mouse ⟍ over this box and then press the left button.

To continue, refer to the next page.

CHANGE FONT FACE

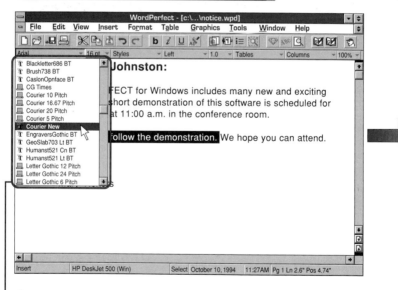

◆ A list of the available font faces appears.

3 Move the mouse ⬚ over the font face you want to use (example: **Courier New**) and then press the left button.

Note: To view all of the available font faces, use the scroll bar. For more information, refer to page 28.

Font faces
can vary from
one computer to
another.

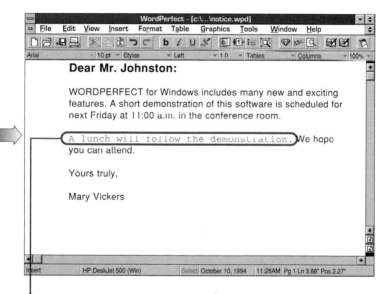

◆ The text you selected
changes to the new font
face.

*Note: To deselect text, move the
mouse I outside the selected area
and then press the left button.*

◆ To select a different font
face, repeat steps **1** to **3**.

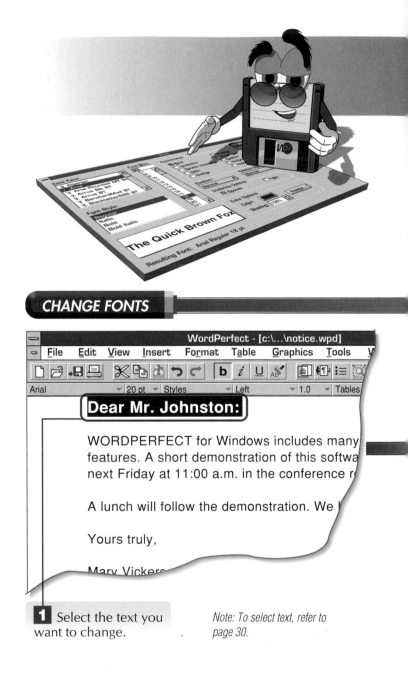

CHANGE FONTS

WordPerfect - [c:\...\notice.wpd]

File   Edit   View   Insert   Format   Table   Graphics   Tools   V

Arial   ▼ 20 pt ▼ Styles   ▼ Left   ▼ 1.0 ▼ Tables

Dear Mr. Johnston:

WORDPERFECT for Windows includes many
features. A short demonstration of this softwa
next Friday at 11:00 a.m. in the conference r

A lunch will follow the demonstration. We

Yours truly,

Mary Vickers

1 Select the text you
want to change.

*Note: To select text, refer to
page 30.*

You can use
the Font dialog box
to change the design
and size of characters
in your document at
the same time.

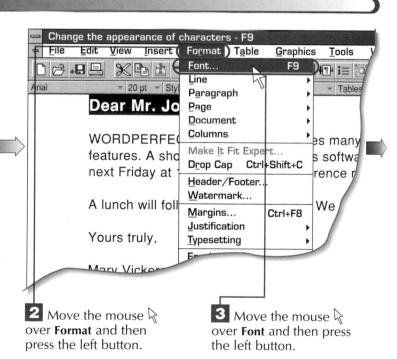

2 Move the mouse ↖
over **Format** and then
press the left button.

3 Move the mouse ↖
over **Font** and then press
the left button.

To continue, refer to the next page.

CHANGE FONTS

You can use these appearance options to emphasize text in your document.

CHANGE FONTS (CONTINUED)

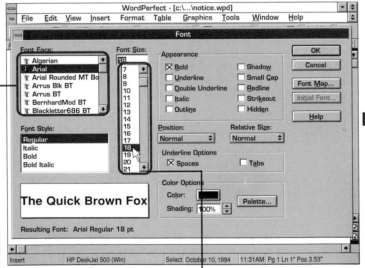

◆ The **Font** dialog box appears.

4 Move the mouse ⤢ over the font face you want to use (example: **Arial**) and then press the left button.

5 Move the mouse ⤢ over the font size you want to use (example: **18**) and then press the left button.

Note: To view more font faces or sizes, use the scroll bar. For more information, refer to page 28.

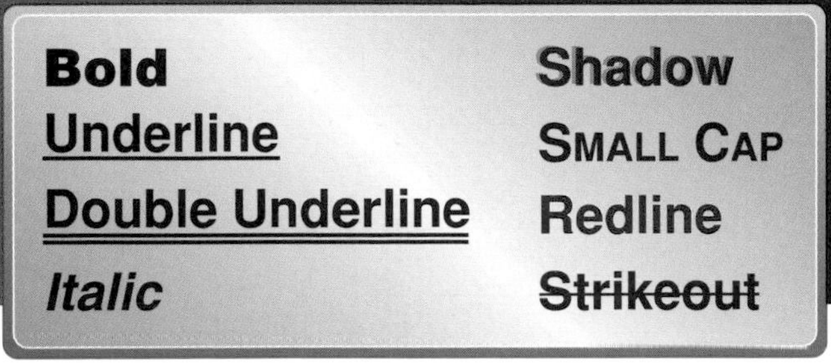
Bold
Underline
Double Underline
Italic
Shadow
SMALL CAP
Redline
Strikeout

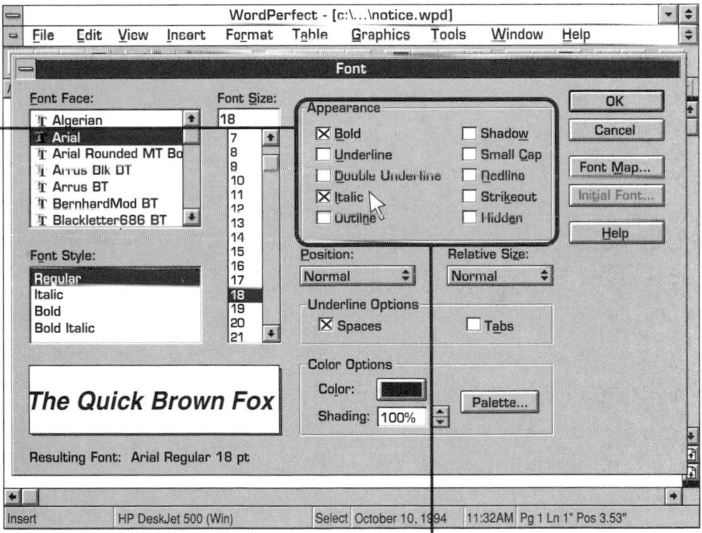
WordPerfect - [c:\...\notice.wpd]
File Edit View Insert Format Table Graphics Tools Window Help
Font
Font Face:
Algerian
Arial
Arial Rounded MT Bo
Arrus Blk BT
Arrus BT
BernhardMod BT
Blackletter686 BT
Font Size:
18
Appearance
Bold
Underline
Double Underline
Italic
Outline
Shadow
Small Cap
Redline
Strikeout
Hidden
OK
Cancel
Font Map...
Initial Font...
Help
Font Style:
Regular
Italic
Bold
Bold Italic
Position:
Normal
Relative Size:
Normal
Underline Options
Spaces
Tabs
Color Options
Color:
Shading: 100%
Palette...
The Quick Brown Fox
Resulting Font: Arial Regular 18 pt
Insert
HP DeskJet 500 (Win)
Select October 10, 1994 11:32AM Pg 1 Ln 1" Pos 3.53"

6 Move the mouse ⇖ over an appearance option you want to use and then press the left button (☐ changes to ☒).

7 Repeat step **6** for each appearance option you want to use.

To continue, refer to the next page.

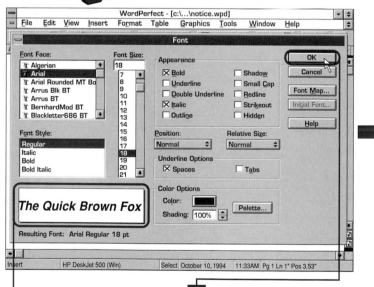

CHANGE FONTS (CONTINUED)

◆ This area displays a sample of the options you selected.

8 Move the mouse ↖ over **OK** and then press the left button.

> Changing the font of text lets you turn a dull, lifeless letter into an interesting, attractive document.

WordPerfect - [c:\...\notice.wpd]

File   Edit   View   Insert   Format   Table   Graphics   Tools

Arial   ▾ 16 pt ▾ Styles   ▾ Left   ▾ 1.0   ▾ Tables

Dear Mr. Johnston:

WORDPERFECT for Windows includes many features. A short demonstration of this softwa next Friday at 11:00 a.m. in the conference r

A lunch will follow the demonstration. We

Yours truly,

Mary Vicker

◆ The text you selected displays the font changes.

Note: To deselect text, move the mouse I outside the selected area and then press the left button.

155

INSERT SPECIAL CHARACTERS

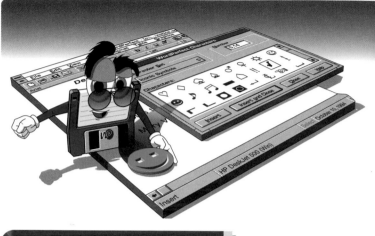

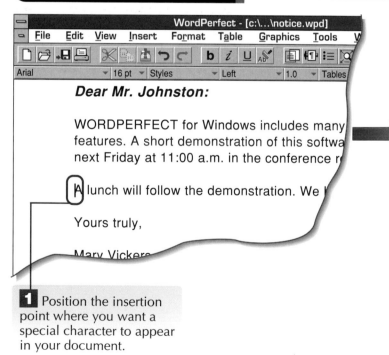

1 Position the insertion point where you want a special character to appear in your document.

156

You can insert characters into your document that do not appear on your keyboard.

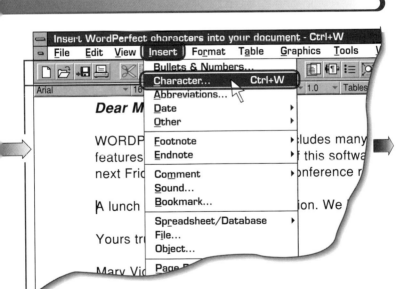

File Edit View Insert Format Table Graphics Tools

Arial ▾ 16

Bullets & Numbers...
Character...   Ctrl+W
Abbreviations...
Date   ▸
Other   ▸

Footnote   ▸
Endnote   ▸

Comment   ▸
Sound...
Bookmark...

Spreadsheet/Database   ▸
File...
Object...

Page

Dear M

WORDP ...ludes many
features ...f this softwa
next Frid ...onference r

A lunch ...ion. We

Yours tr

Mary Vid

2 Move the mouse ⬚ over **Insert** and then press the left button.

3 Move the mouse ⬚ over **Character** and then press the left button.

◆ The **WordPerfect Characters** dialog box appears.

To continue, refer to the next page.

157

INSERT SPECIAL CHARACTERS

WordPerfect offers fourteen different sets of characters.

WordPerfect - [c:\...\notice.wpd]

File Edit View Insert Format Table Graphics Tools Window Help

Arial   16 pt   Styles   Left   1.0   Tables   Columns   100%

Dear Mr. Johnston:

WORDPERFECT for Windows includes many new and exciting
features. A short de
next Friday at 11:0(

A lunch will follow t

Yours truly,

Mary Vickers

WordPerfect Characters

Character Set

Typographic Symbols

Number

4,0

Characters:

● ○ ■ ● ★ ¶
§ ¡ ¿ « » £
¥ P+ ƒ ª º ½

Insert   Insert and Close   Close   Help

Insert   HP DeskJet 500 (Win)   Select October 10, 1994   11:37AM Pg 1 Ln 2.56" Pos 1"

◆ This area displays
characters that you can
insert into your document.

◆ This area displays the
name of the current set of
characters.

4 To display another set
of characters, move the
mouse ⇖ over this box and
then press and hold down
the left button.

WordPerfect - [c:\...\notice.wpd]

File   Edit   View   Insert   Format   Table   Graphics   Tools   Window   Help

Arial   16 pt   Styles   Left   1.0   Tables   Columns   100%

Dear Mr. Johnston:

WORDPERFECT for   now and exciting
features. A short de   Characters
next Friday at 11:00

                        ✓ Typographic Symbols   Number
                        Iconic Symbols   4,0
A lunch will follow t   Math/Scientific
                        Math/Scientific Ext.

Yours truly,   Greek
                        Hebrew   ★   ¶
                        Cyrillic
Mary Vickers   Japanese   ≫   £
                        User-Defined
                        Arabic   o   ½
                        Arabic Script

                        ASCII
                        Multinational
                        Phonetic
                        Box Drawing

                        Insert   Insert and Close   Close   Help

Insert   HP DeskJet 500 (Win)   Select October 10, 1994   11:38AM Pg 1 Ln 2.56" Pos 1"

5 Still holding down the
button, move the mouse
over the character set you
want to view. Then release
the button.

To continue, refer to the next page.

INSERT SPECIAL CHARACTERS

◆ The characters in the new set appear.

6 Move the mouse ⬉ over the character you want to place in your document and then press the left button.

7 Move the mouse ⬉ over **Insert and Close** and then press the left button.

You can
add characters
such as ☺, ♫ or √
to liven up your
documents.

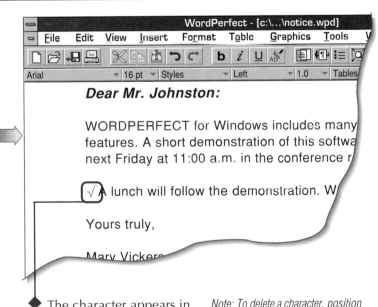

◆ The character appears in
your document.

*Note: To delete a character, position
the insertion point to the left of the
character and then press* **Delete** *.*

JUSTIFY TEXT

- ◆ Right
- ◆ Center
- ◆ Left
- ◆ Full
- ◆ All

JUSTIFY TEXT

WordPerfect - [c:\...\notice.wpd]

| File | Edit | View | Insert | Format | Table | Graphics | Tools | W |

Arial | 18 pt | Styles | Left | 1.0 | Tables

Left
Right
Center
Full
All

Dear Mr. Johnston:

WORDPERFECT for Wi‌ des many
features. A short demonstration of this softwa
next Friday at 11:00 a.m. in the conference r

A lunch will follow the demonstration. We

Yours truly,

Mary Vicke

1 Position the insertion point where you want the new justification to begin.

Note: To change the justification of a section of text, select the text you want to change. To select text, refer to page 30.

2 Move the mouse over this box and then press the left button.

3 Move the mouse over the justification option you want to use (example: **Center**) and then press the left button.

162

You can enhance the appearance of your document by justifying text in different ways. WordPerfect offers several justification options.

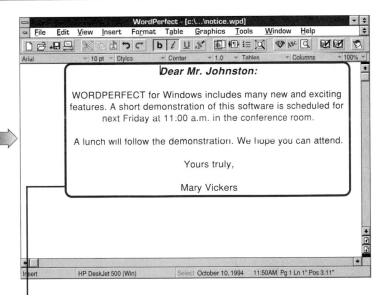

◆ The paragraph containing the insertion point and all text that follows display the new justification.

*Note: To return to the original justification, repeat steps **1** to **3**, selecting **Left** in step **3**.*

CHANGE LINE SPACING

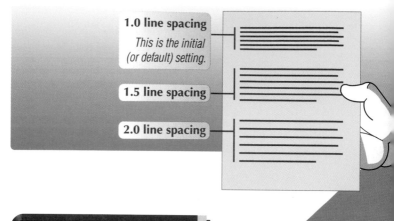

1.0 line spacing
This is the initial (or default) setting.

1.5 line spacing

2.0 line spacing

CHANGE LINE SPACING

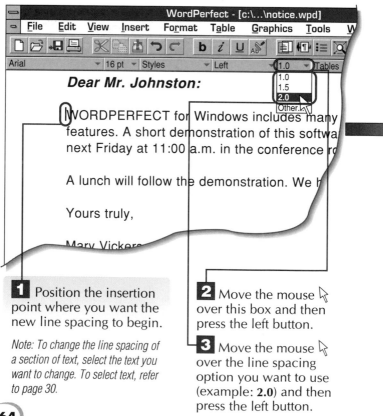

WordPerfect - [c:\...\notice.wpd]

File Edit View Insert Format Table Graphics Tools W

Arial ▼ 16 pt ▼ Styles ▼ Left 1.0 ▼ Tables

1.0
1.5
2.0
Other.

Dear Mr. Johnston:

WORDPERFECT for Windows includes many features. A short demonstration of this softwa next Friday at 11:00 a.m. in the conference ro

A lunch will follow the demonstration. We h

Yours truly,

Mary Vickers

1 Position the insertion point where you want the new line spacing to begin.

Note: To change the line spacing of a section of text, select the text you want to change. To select text, refer to page 30.

2 Move the mouse ↕ over this box and then press the left button.

3 Move the mouse ↕ over the line spacing option you want to use (example: **2.0**) and then press the left button.

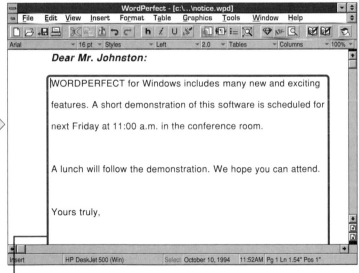

◆ The paragraph containing the insertion point and all text that follows display the new line spacing.

Note: To return to the original line spacing, repeat steps **1** *to* **3**, *selecting* **1.0** *in step* **3**.

DELETE A TAB

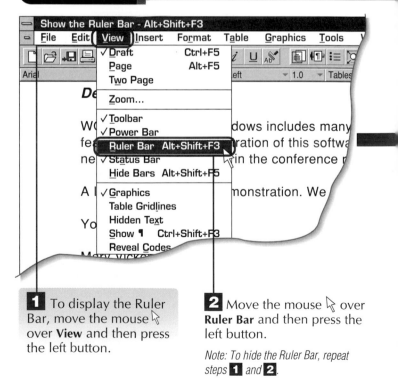

DELETE A TAB

Show the Ruler Bar - Alt+Shift+F3

File **Edit** **View** **Insert** **Format** **Table** **Graphics** **Tools**

✓	Draft	Ctrl+F5
	Page	Alt+F5
	Two Page	
	Zoom...	
✓	Toolbar	
✓	Power Bar	
	Ruler Bar	Alt+Shift+F3
✓	Status Bar	
	Hide Bars	Alt+Shift+F5
✓	Graphics	
	Table Gridlines	
	Hidden Text	
	Show ¶	Ctrl+Shift+F3
	Reveal Codes	

Arial ... Left ... 1.0 ... Tables

De

Wo ... dows includes many
fe ... ration of this softwa
ne ... in the conference

A l ... monstration. We

Yo

1 To display the Ruler
Bar, move the mouse ⬉
over **View** and then press
the left button.

2 Move the mouse ⬉ over
Ruler Bar and then press the
left button.

*Note: To hide the Ruler Bar, repeat
steps* **1** *and* **2**.

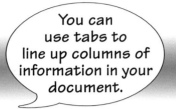

You can
use tabs to
line up columns of
information in your
document.

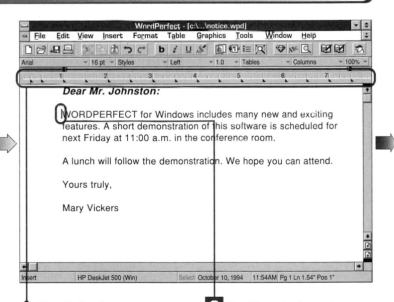

◆ The Ruler Bar appears
displaying the current tab
locations. WordPerfect
initially sets a left tab (◣)
at every half inch.

3 Position the insertion
point where you want the
new tab settings to begin.

To continue, refer to the next page.

167

DELETE A TAB

To ensure your document prints correctly, use tabs rather than spaces to line up columns of text.

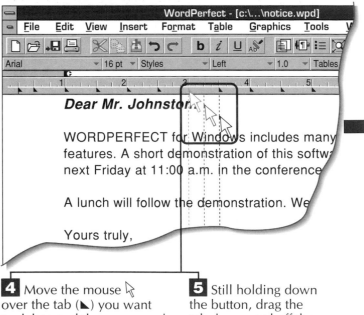

DELETE A TAB (CONTINUED)

4 Move the mouse ⤷ over the tab (▲) you want to delete and then press and hold down the left button.

5 Still holding down the button, drag the tab downward off the Ruler Bar.

◆ In this example, spaces were used to line up columns.

Last Name	First Name	Address	City	State	Zip Code
Appleton	Jill	456 John Street	Portland	OR	97526
DeVries	Monica	12 Willow Avenue	Los Angeles	CA	90032
Grossi	Rob	23 Riverbead Road	Seattle	WA	98109
Knill	Mark	97 Speers Road	Denver	CO	80207
g	Justin	15 Lakeshore Drive	Atlanta	GA	30367
ey	Jennifer	34 Kerr Street	Provo	UT	84604
		56 Devon Road	Dallas	TX	75236

◆ In this example, tabs were used to line up columns.

Last Name	First Name	Address	City	State	Zip Code
Appleton	Jill	456 John Street	Portland	OR	97526
DeVries	Monica	12 Willow Avenue	Los Angeles	CA	90032
Grossi	Rob	23 Riverbead Road	Seattle	WA	98109
Knill	Mark	97 Speers Road	Denver	CO	80207
Leung	Justin	15 Lakeshore Drive	Atlanta	GA	30367
Matwey	Jennifer	34 Kerr Street	Provo	UT	84604
Smith	Albert	56 Devon Road	Dallas	TX	75236
Smith	Betty	111 Linton Street	Los Angeles	CA	90071
Smith	Carol	36 Ford Drive	Santa Clara	CA	95054
Anderson	David	55 Kennedy Road	Buffalo	NY	14213

WordPerfect - [c:\...\notice.wpd]

File   Edit   View   Insert   Format   Table   Graphics   Tools

Arial   ▼ 16 pt ▼ Styles   ▼ Left   ▼ 1.0   ▼ Tables

1   2   3   4   5

Dear Mr. Johnston:

WORDPERFECT for Windows includes many features. A short demonstration of this softw next Friday at 11:00 a.m. in the conference

A lunch will follow the demonstration. We

Yours truly,

6 Release the button and the tab disappears.

◆ Repeat steps **4** to **6** for each tab you want to delete.

ADD A TAB

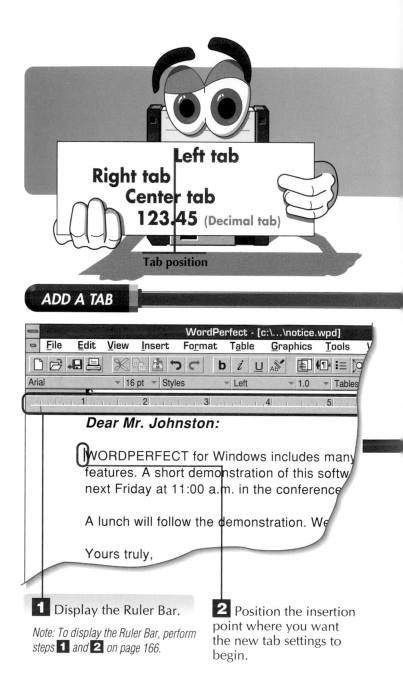

Left tab

Right tab

Center tab

123.45 (Decimal tab)

Tab position

ADD A TAB

WordPerfect - [c:\...\notice.wpd]

File　Edit　View　Insert　Format　Table　Graphics　Tools

Arial　▼ 16 pt ▼ Styles　▼ Left　▼ 1.0 ▼ Tables

Dear Mr. Johnston:

WORDPERFECT for Windows includes many
features. A short demonstration of this softw
next Friday at 11:00 a.m. in the conference

A lunch will follow the demonstration. We

Yours truly,

1 Display the Ruler Bar.

*Note: To display the Ruler Bar, perform
steps **1** and **2** on page 166.*

2 Position the insertion
point where you want
the new tab settings to
begin.

WordPerfect offers four types of tabs to help you line up text in your document.

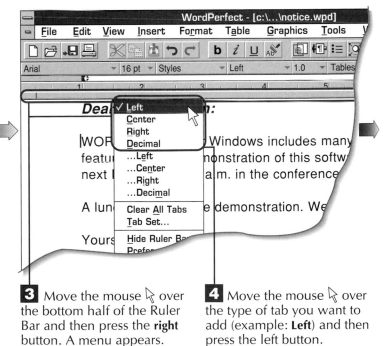

3 Move the mouse ⇗ over the bottom half of the Ruler Bar and then press the **right** button. A menu appears.

4 Move the mouse ⇗ over the type of tab you want to add (example: **Left**) and then press the left button.

To continue, refer to the next page.

171

ADD A TAB

After you have set tabs, you can use them to quickly move the insertion point across your screen.

WordPerfect - [c:\...\notice.wpd]

File   Edit   View   Insert   Format   Table   Graphics   Tools

Arial   ▼ 16 pt ▼ Styles   ▼ Left   ▼ 1.0 ▼ Tables

Dear Mr. Johnston:

WORDPERFECT for Windows includes many features. A short demonstration of this softw next Friday at 11:00 a.m. in the conference

A lunch will follow the demonstration. We

Yours truly,

5 Move the mouse ⬚ over the position on the Ruler Bar where you want to add the tab and then press the left button.

◆ The new tab setting appears on the Ruler Bar.

172

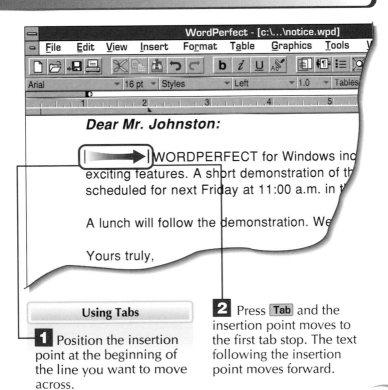

Dear Mr. Johnston:

WORDPERFECT for Windows inc
exciting features. A short demonstration of th
scheduled for next Friday at 11:00 a.m. in t

A lunch will follow the demonstration. We

Yours truly,

Using Tabs

1 Position the insertion point at the beginning of the line you want to move across.

2 Press Tab and the insertion point moves to the first tab stop. The text following the insertion point moves forward.

173

INDENT A PARAGRAPH

You can use the Indent feature to emphasize paragraphs in your document.

INDENT A PARAGRAPH

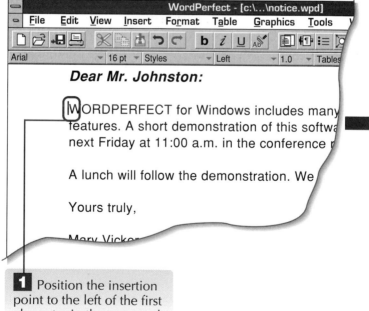

WordPerfect - [c:\...\notice.wpd]

File   Edit   View   Insert   Format   Table   Graphics   Tools

Arial   16 pt   Styles   Left   1.0   Tables

Dear Mr. Johnston:

[M]ORDPERFECT for Windows includes many
features. A short demonstration of this softwa
next Friday at 11:00 a.m. in the conference

A lunch will follow the demonstration. We

Yours truly,

Mary Vicker

1 Position the insertion
point to the left of the first
character in the paragraph
you want to indent.

174

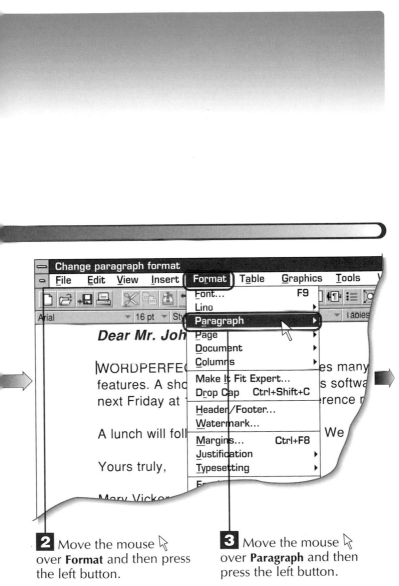

Change paragraph format

| File | Edit | View | Insert | Format | Table | Graphics | Tools |

Font...   F9
Lino
Paragraph
Page
Document
Columns
Make It Fit Expert...
Drop Cap   Ctrl+Shift+C
Header/Footer...
Watermark...
Margins...   Ctrl+F8
Justification
Typesetting

Arial   ▼ 16 pt ▼ Sty   ▼ Tables

Dear Mr. Joh

WORDPERFE   es many
features. A sho   s softwa
next Friday at   erence

A lunch will foll   We

Yours truly,

Mary Vicke

2 Move the mouse ⌖ over **Format** and then press the left button.

3 Move the mouse ⌖ over **Paragraph** and then press the left button.

To continue, refer to the next page.

175

INDENT A PARAGRAPH

Indent

Hanging Indent

Double Indent

1

INDENT A PARAGRAPH (CONTINUED)

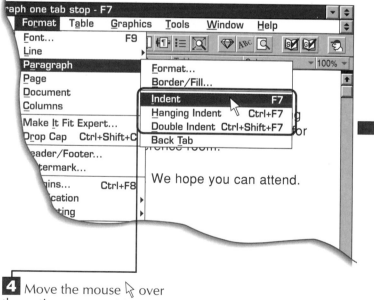

raph one tab stop - F7

| Format | Table | Graphics | Tools | Window | Help |

Font... F9
Line
Paragraph
Page
Document
Columns

Make It Fit Expert...
Drop Cap Ctrl+Shift+C

eader/Footer...
termark...
ins... Ctrl+F8
cation
ting

Format...
Border/Fill...

Indent F7
Hanging Indent Ctrl+F7
Double Indent Ctrl+Shift+F7
Back Tab

100%

We hope you can attend.

4 Move the mouse ⍾ over
the option you want to use
(example: **Indent**) and then
press the left button.

WordPerfect
offers three indent
options that you can
choose from.

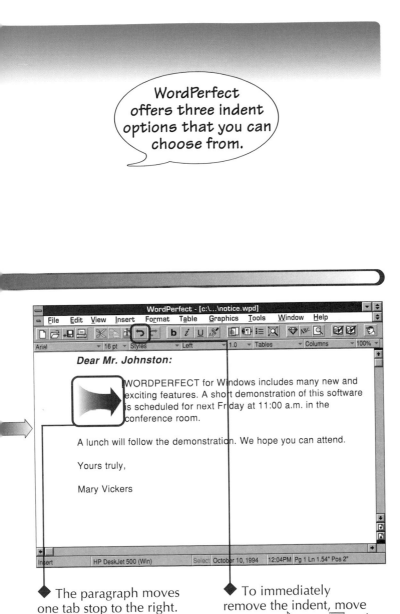

◆ The paragraph moves
one tab stop to the right.

◆ To immediately
remove the indent, move
the mouse ⟨ over ⟲ and
then press the left button.

ADD BULLETS AND NUMBERS

ADD BULLETS AND NUMBERS

1 Select the paragraphs you want to display bullets or numbers.

Note: To select text, refer to page 30.

You can separate items in a list by beginning each item with a bullet or number.

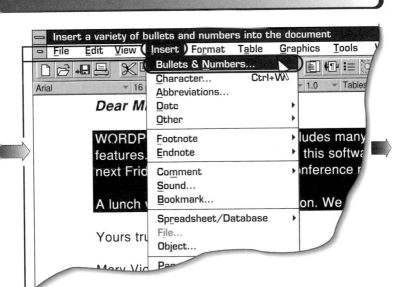

Insert a variety of bullets and numbers into the document

| File | Edit | View | Insert | Format | Table | Graphics | Tools |

Bullets & Numbers...
Character...   Ctrl+W
Abbreviations...
Date   ▶
Other   ▶

Footnote   ▶
Endnote   ▶

Comment   ▶
Sound...
Bookmark...

Spreadsheet/Database   ▶
File...
Object...

Arial   16

Dear M

WORDP   ludes many
features.   this softwa
next Frid   nference r

A lunch   on. We

Yours tru

Mary Vic

2 Move the mouse ⌖ over **Insert** and then press the left button.

3 Move the mouse ⌖ over **Bullets & Numbers** and then press the left button.

◆ The **Bullets & Numbers** dialog box appears.

To continue, refer to the next page.

ADD BULLETS AND NUMBERS

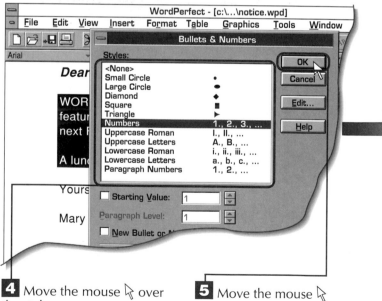

WordPerfect - [c:\...\notice.wpd]

File   Edit   View   Insert   Format   Table   Graphics   Tools   Window

Bullets & Numbers

Arial

Dear

Styles:

<None>	
Small Circle	•
Large Circle	●
Diamond	◆
Square	■
Triangle	▶
Numbers	1., 2., 3., ...
Uppercase Roman	I., II., ...
Uppercase Letters	A., B., ...
Lowercase Roman	i., ii., iii., ...
Lowercase Letters	a., b., c., ...
Paragraph Numbers	1., 2., ...

OK

Cancel

Edit...

Help

WOR
featur
next

A lun

Yours

☐ Starting Value: 1

Mary

Paragraph Level: 1

☐ New Bullet or

4 Move the mouse � over the style you want to use (example: **Numbers**) and then press the left button.

5 Move the mouse � over **OK** and then press the left button.

180

> Numbers are useful for items in a specific order, such as a recipe. Bullets are useful for items in no particular order, such as a list of goals.

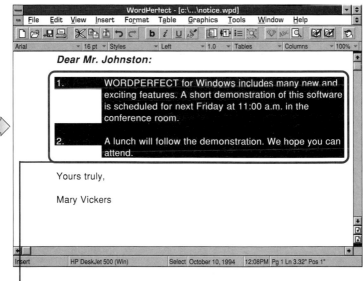

◆ The bullets or numbers appear in your document.

*Note: To remove the bullets or numbers, repeat steps **1** to **5** starting on page 178, selecting **<None>** in step **4**.*

ADD BORDERS AND SHADING

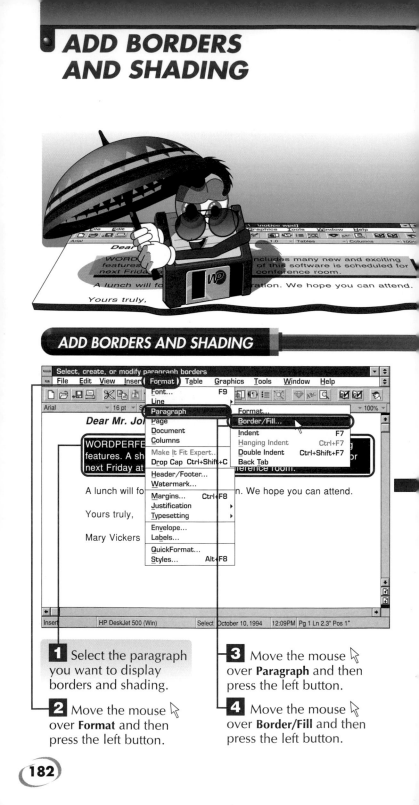

ADD BORDERS AND SHADING

Select, create, or modify paragraph borders

File   Edit   View   Insert   Format   Table   Graphics   Tools   Window   Help

Arial   16 pt

Font...   F9
Line
Paragraph   Format...
Page   Border/Fill...
Document   Indent   F7
Columns   Hanging Indent   Ctrl+F7
Make It Fit Expert..   Double Indent   Ctrl+Shift+F7
Drop Cap Ctrl+Shift+C   Back Tab
Header/Footer...
Watermark...
Margins...   Ctrl+F8
Justification
Typesetting
Envelope...
Labels...
QuickFormat...
Styles...   Alt+F8

Dear Mr. Jo

WORDPERFE...
features. A sh...
next Friday at...   ...erence room.

A lunch will fo...   ...n. We hope you can attend.

Yours truly,

Mary Vickers

Insert   HP DeskJet 500 (Win)   Select   October 10, 1994   12:09PM Pg 1 Ln 2.3" Pos 1"

1 Select the paragraph you want to display borders and shading.

2 Move the mouse ⌖ over **Format** and then press the left button.

3 Move the mouse ⌖ over **Paragraph** and then press the left button.

4 Move the mouse ⌖ over **Border/Fill** and then press the left button.

182

You can add
borders and shading
to draw attention to
important information
in your document.

◆ The **Paragraph Border** dialog box appears.

5 To add a border, move the mouse ⬀ over this box and then press the left button.

6 Move the mouse ⬀ over the border style you want to use and then press the left button.

To continue, refer to the next page.

183

ADD BORDERS AND SHADING

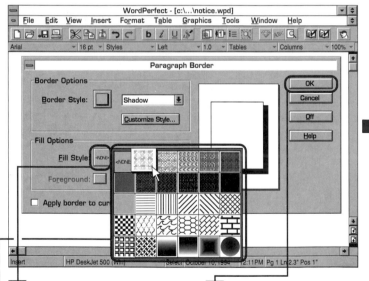

7 To add shading, move the mouse over this box and then press the left button.

8 Move the mouse over the fill style you want to use and then press the left button.

9 Move the mouse over **OK** and then press the left button.

184

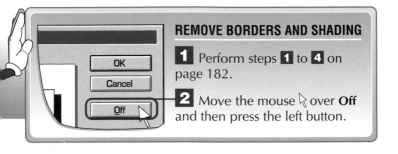

REMOVE BORDERS AND SHADING

1 Perform steps **1** to **4** on page 182.

2 Move the mouse � over **Off** and then press the left button.

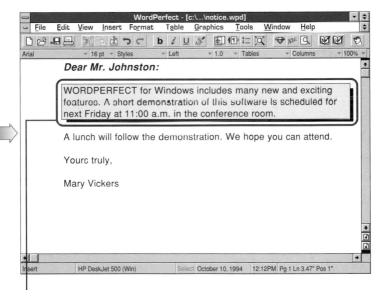

◆ The paragraph displays the border and shading styles you selected.

Note: To deselect a paragraph, move the mouse ⊥ outside the selected area and then press the left button.

If you want
to start a new
page at a specific place
in your document,
you can insert a
page break.

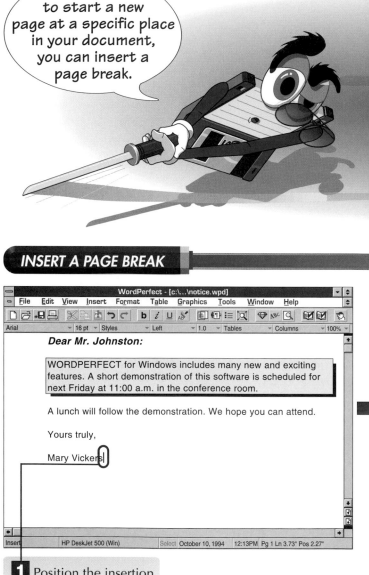

INSERT A PAGE BREAK

1 Position the insertion point where you want to start a new page.

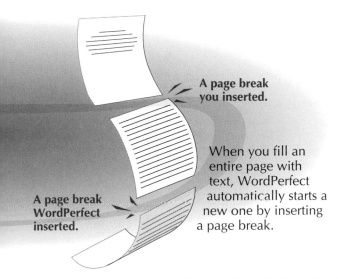

A page break you inserted.

When you fill an entire page with text, WordPerfect automatically starts a new one by inserting a page break.

A page break WordPerfect inserted.

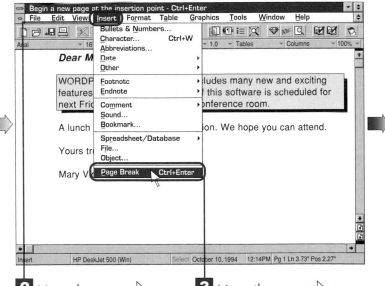

2 Move the mouse ▷ over **Insert** and then press the left button.

3 Move the mouse ▷ over **Page Break** and then press the left button.

To continue, refer to the next page.

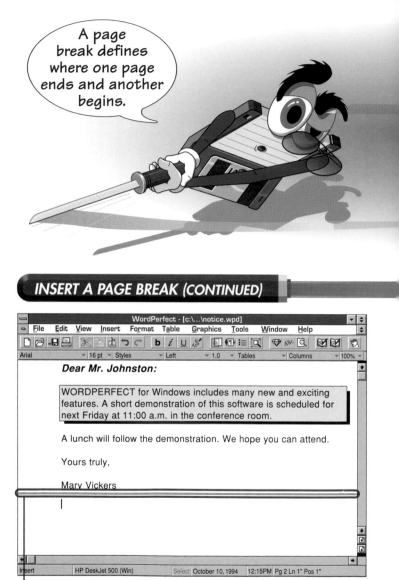

A page break defines where one page ends and another begins.

INSERT A PAGE BREAK (CONTINUED)

◆ A double line appears across your screen. This line defines where one page ends and another begins.

Note: This line will not appear when you print your document.

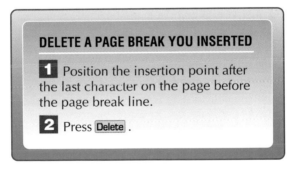

DELETE A PAGE BREAK YOU INSERTED

1 Position the insertion point after the last character on the page before the page break line.

2 Press `Delete`.

CHANGE MARGINS

CHANGE LEFT AND RIGHT MARGINS

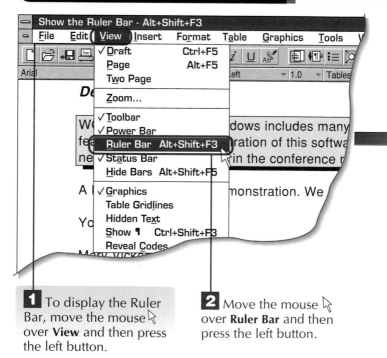

1 To display the Ruler Bar, move the mouse ▷ over **View** and then press the left button.

2 Move the mouse ▷ over **Ruler Bar** and then press the left button.

> A margin is the amount of space between text and an edge of your paper. You can change the margin settings to shorten or lengthen your document.

```
┌─────────────────────────────────────────────────────────────┐
│                WordPerfect - [c:\...\notice.wpd]        ▼ ▲  │
│  File  Edit  View  Insert  Format  Table  Graphics  Tools  Window  Help  ▲ │
│  ┌─┬─┬─┬─┐  ┌─┬─┬─┬─┐ b i U A  ┌─┬─┬─┬─┐  ▽ ABC Q  ☑☑  │
│ Arial        ▼ 18 pt ▼ Styles    ▼ Left   ▼ 1.0  ▼ Tables  ▼ Columns  ▼ 100% ▼│
│   . . . . . 2 . . . 3 . . . 4 . . . 5 . . . 6 . . . 7 . . . │
│                                                              │
│  Dear Mr. Johnston:                                          │
│  ┌─────────────────────────────────────────────────────┐   │
│  │ WORDPERFECT for Windows includes many new and exciting│   │
│  │ features. A short demonstration of this software is scheduled for│
│  │ next Friday at 11:00 a.m. in the conference room.     │   │
│  └─────────────────────────────────────────────────────┘   │
│                                                              │
│  A lunch will follow the demonstration. We hope you can attend.│
│                                                              │
│  Yours truly,                                                │
│                                                              │
│  Mary Vickers                                                │
│                                                              │
│ Insert    HP DeskJet 500 (Win)   Select October 10, 1994  12:17PM Pg 1 Ln 1" Pos 1" │
└─────────────────────────────────────────────────────────────┘
```

◆ The Ruler Bar appears, displaying the left (◀) and right (▶) margin markers.

3 Position the insertion point where you want the new margin(s) to begin.

To continue, refer to the next page.

CHANGE MARGINS

WordPerfect - [c:\...\notice.wpd]

File **Edit** **View** **Insert** **For_mat** **Table** **Graphics** **Tools**

Arial ▼ 18 pt ▼ Styles ▼ Left ▼ 1.0 ▼ Tables

1 | 2 | 3 | 4 | 5 |

Dear Mr. Johnston:

WORDPERFECT for Windows includes many
features. A short demonstration of this softw
next Friday at 11:00 a.m. in the conferenc

A lunch will follow the demonstration. W

Yours truly,

4 Position the mouse ⟍
over the margin marker you
want to move (example: ◖)
and then press and hold
down the left button.

5 Still holding down the
button, drag the margin
marker to a new position
(example: **2 inches**).

*Note: The dotted line indicates the
new margin setting.*

> WordPerfect
> initially sets the
> left and right margins
> in your document at
> one inch.

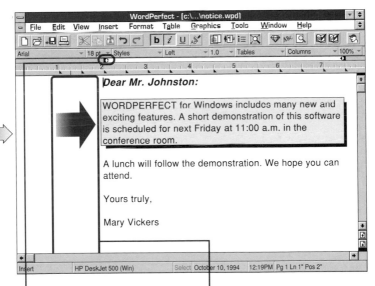

6 Release the button and the margin marker moves to the new position.

◆ The paragraph containing the insertion point and all text that follows display the new margin(s).

Note: To hide the Ruler Bar, repeat steps 1 and 2 on page 190.

193

CHANGE MARGINS

You can change the top and bottom margins to accommodate letterhead or other specialty paper.

CHANGE TOP AND BOTTOM MARGINS

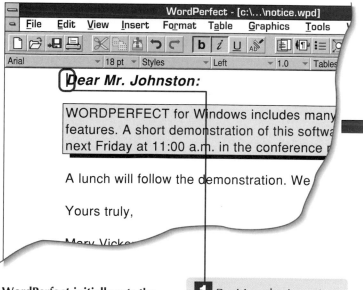

WordPerfect - [c:\...\notice.wpd]

File   Edit   View   Insert   Format   Table   Graphics   Tools

Arial   18 pt   Styles   Left   1.0   Tables

Dear Mr. Johnston:

WORDPERFECT for Windows includes many features. A short demonstration of this softwa next Friday at 11:00 a.m. in the conference r

A lunch will follow the demonstration. We

Yours truly,

Mary Vicke

WordPerfect initially sets the top and bottom margins in your document at one inch.

1 Position the insertion point anywhere on the page where you want the new margin(s) to begin.

194

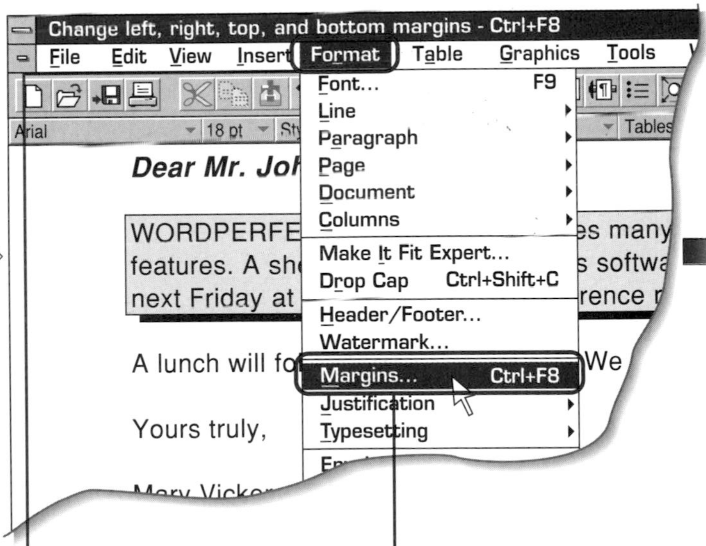

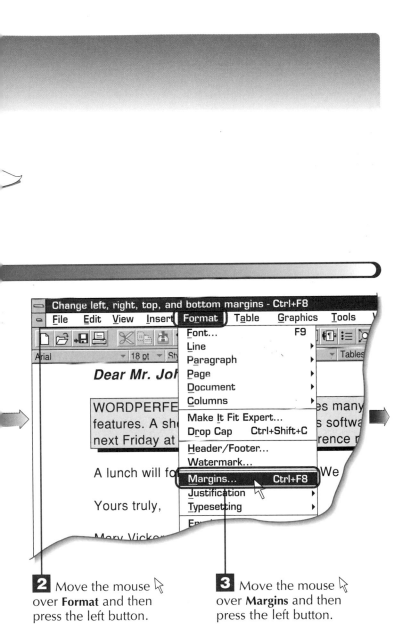

2 Move the mouse over **Format** and then press the left button.

3 Move the mouse over **Margins** and then press the left button.

To continue, refer to the next page.

CHANGE MARGINS

CHANGE MARGINS (CONTINUED)

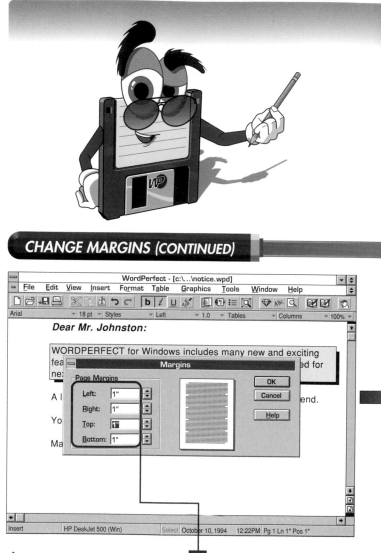

◆ The **Margins** dialog box appears.

Note: You can use this dialog box to change the left, right, top and bottom margins.

4 Press **Tab** until you highlight the number beside the margin you want to change (example: **Top**).

VIEW MARGINS

You can use to display an entire page. This lets you view the margins in your document.

1 Move the mouse ⌖ over and then press the left button.

*Note: Repeat step **1** to return to the original view.*

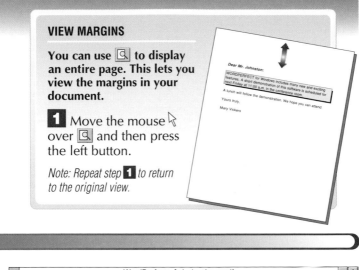

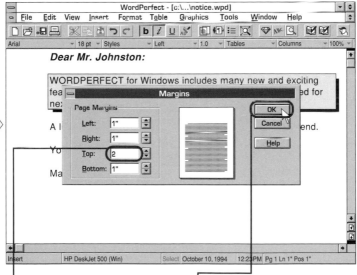

5 Type the new margin in inches (example: **2**).

*Note: Repeat steps **4** and **5** for each margin you want to change.*

6 Move the mouse ⌖ over **OK** and then press the left button.

◆ The page containing the insertion point and all pages that follow change to the new margin(s).

CENTER A PAGE

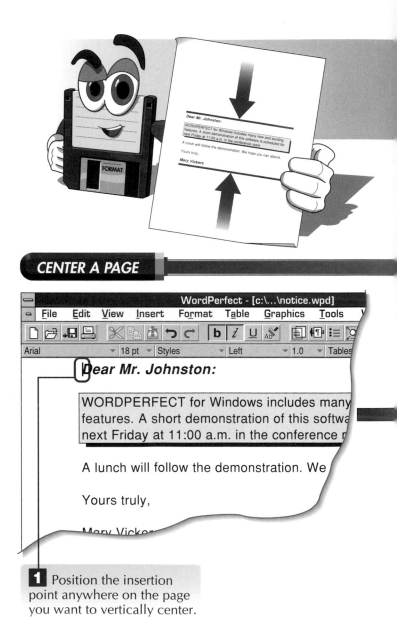

1 Position the insertion point anywhere on the page you want to vertically center.

> You can vertically center text on a page. This is useful for creating title pages or short memos.

Center one or more pages

File   Edit   View   Inser   Format   Table   Graphics   Tools   Window   Help

Arial   18 pt   St

Dear Mr. Jo

WORDPERFE
features. A sh
next Friday at

A lunch will fo

Yours truly,

Mary Vickers

Format menu:
Font...   F9
Line
Paragraph
Page   ▸   Center...
Document   Suppress...
Columns   Delay Codes...
Make It Fit Expert...   Force Page...
Drop Cap   Ctrl+Shift+C   Keep Text Together...
Header/Footer...   Border/Fill...
Watermark...   Numbering...
Margins...   Ctrl+F8   Subdivide Page...
Justification   Binding/Duplex...
Typesetting   Paper Size...
Envelope...
Labels...
QuickFormat...
Styles...   Alt+F8

xciting
uled for

ttend.

Insert   HP DeskJet 500 (Win)   Select   October 10, 1994   12:25PM Pg 1 Ln 1" Pos 1"

2 Move the mouse ⇧ over **Format** and then press the left button.

3 Move the mouse ⇧ over **Page** and then press the left button.

4 Move the mouse ⇧ over **Center** and then press the left button.

To continue, refer to the next page.

199

CENTER A PAGE

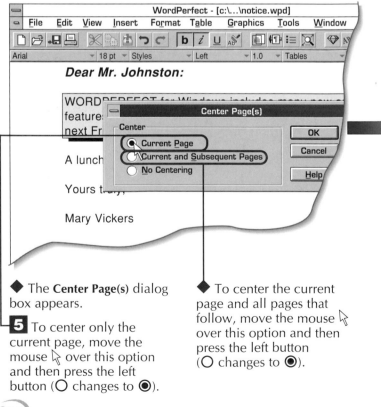

◆ The **Center Page(s)** dialog box appears.

5 To center only the current page, move the mouse ⊾ over this option and then press the left button (○ changes to ◉).

◆ To center the current page and all pages that follow, move the mouse ⊾ over this option and then press the left button (○ changes to ◉).

VIEW CENTERED PAGE

You can use 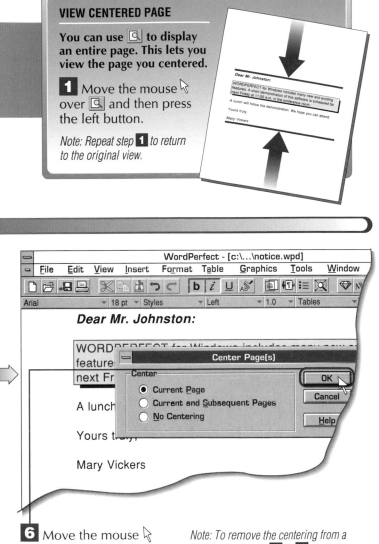 to display an entire page. This lets you view the page you centered.

1 Move the mouse over and then press the left button.

*Note: Repeat step **1** to return to the original view.*

Dear Mr. Johnston:

WORDPERFECT for Windows includes many new and exciting features. A short demonstration of this software is scheduled for next Friday at 11:00 a.m. in the conference room.

A lunch will follow the demonstration. We hope you can attend.

Yours truly,

Mary Vickers

WordPerfect - [c:\...\notice.wpd]

File   Edit   View   Insert   Format   Table   Graphics   Tools   Window

Arial   18 pt   Styles   Left   1.0   Tables

Dear Mr. Johnston:

WORDPERFECT for Windows includes many new a
feature
next Fr

Center Page(s)

Center
- Current Page
- Current and Subsequent Pages
- No Centering

OK
Cancel
Help

A lunch

Yours truly,

Mary Vickers

6 Move the mouse over **OK** and then press the left button.

*Note: To remove the centering from a page, repeat steps **1** to **6** starting on page 198, selecting **Turn Centering Off** in step **5**.*

ADD PAGE NUMBERS

ADD PAGE NUMBERS

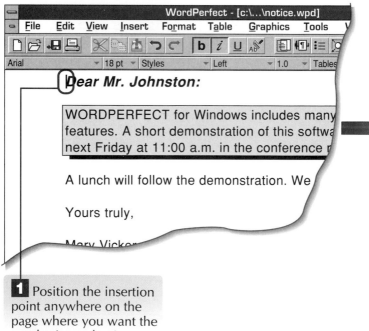

1 Position the insertion point anywhere on the page where you want the numbering to begin.

You can have WordPerfect number the pages in your document.

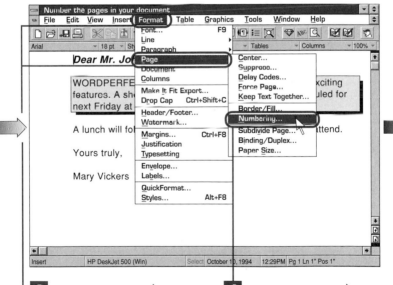

2 Move the mouse ⟶ over **Format** and then press the left button.

3 Move the mouse ⟶ over **Page** and then press the left button.

4 Move the mouse ⟶ over **Numbering** and then press the left button.

To continue, refer to the next page.

ADD PAGE NUMBERS

ADD PAGE NUMBERS (CONTINUED)

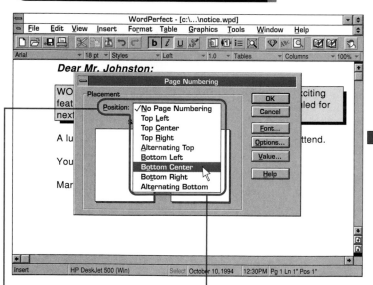

◆ The **Page Numbering** dialog box appears.

5 Move the mouse ❆ over the box beside **Position:** and then press and hold down the left button.

6 Still holding down the button, move the mouse ❆ over the position where you want the page numbers to appear (example: **Bottom Center**).

204

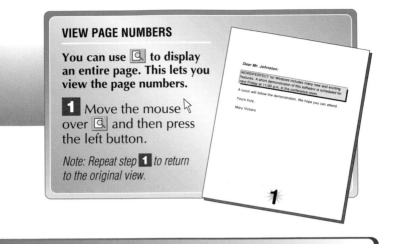

VIEW PAGE NUMBERS

You can use ▢ to display an entire page. This lets you view the page numbers.

1 Move the mouse ▷ over ▢ and then press the left button.

*Note: Repeat step **1** to return to the original view.*

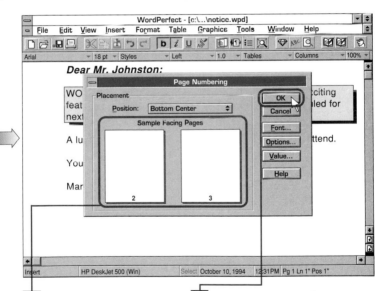

7 Release the button and a sample of the page numbering appears.

8 Move the mouse ▷ over **OK** and then press the left button.

*Note: To remove the page numbers, repeat steps **1** to **8** starting on page 202, selecting **No Page Numbering** in step **6**.*

ADD HEADERS OR FOOTERS

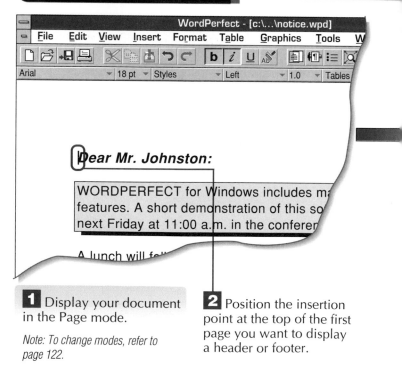

1 Display your document in the Page mode.

Note: To change modes, refer to page 122.

2 Position the insertion point at the top of the first page you want to display a header or footer.

You can add a header or footer to your document to display such information as the date or your company name.

Create and edit headers and footers

File Edit View Insert Format Table Graphics Tools W

Arial   ▾ 18 pt ▾ Styl

Font...   F9
Line
Paragraph
Page
Document
Columns

Make It Fit Expert...
Drop Cap   Ctrl+Shift+C
Header/Footer...
Watermark...
Margins...   Ctrl+F8
Justification
Typesetting
Envelo

Dear Mr. Joh

WORDPERFE
features. A sho
next Friday at

A lunch will fo

3 Move the mouse ⌖ over **Format** and then press the left button.

4 Move the mouse ⌖ over **Header/Footer** and then press the left button.

◆ The **Headers/Footers** dialog box appears.

To continue, refer to the next page.

ADD HEADERS OR FOOTERS

◆ **Header**

◆ **Footer**

ADD HEADERS OR FOOTERS (CONTINUED)

WordPerfect - [c:\...\notice.wpd]

File   Edit   View   Insert   Format   Table   Graphics   Tools   Window   Help

Arial   ▼ 18 pt ▼ Styles   ▼ Left   ▼ 1.0   ▼ Tables   ▼ Columns   ▼ 100% ▼

Dear Mr. Joh

Headers/Footers

Select
- ● Header **A**
- ○ Header **B**
- ○ Footer **A**
- ○ Footer **B**

Create
Edit
Discontinue
Cancel
Help

WORDPERFE... new and exciting
features. A sho... e is scheduled for
next Friday at ... m.

A lunch will fol... you can attend.

Yours truly,

Mary Vickers

Insert   HP DeskJet 500 (Win)   Select October 10, 1994   12:34PM Pg 1 Ln 1" Pos 1"

5 Move the mouse ⟍ over the header or footer you want to create (example: **Header A**) and then press the left button.

*Note: You can create two headers and two footers (**A** and **B**) for each page.*

6 Move the mouse ⟍ over **Create** and then press the left button.

208

A header displays information at the top of a page. A footer displays information at the bottom of a page.

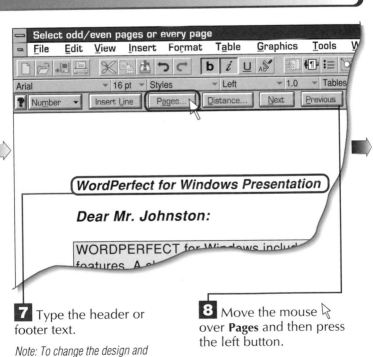

7 Type the header or footer text.

Note: To change the design and size of the text, refer to page 150.

8 Move the mouse over **Pages** and then press the left button.

To continue, refer to the next page.

ADD HEADERS
OR FOOTERS

```
WordPerfect - [c:\...\notice.wpd - Header A]
File  Edit  View  Insert  Format  Table  Graphics  Tools  Window  Help
```

Arial   ▾ 16 pt ▾ Styles   ▾ Left   ▾ 1.0 ▾ Tables   ▾ Columns   ▾ 100% ▾

Number ▾   Insert Line   Pages...   Distance...   Next   Previous   Close

WordPerfect f

Dear Mr. Joh

Pages

Place On
- ○ Odd Pages
- ○ Even Pages
- ● Every Page

OK
Cancel
Help

WORDPERFE[...] new and exciting
features. A sho[...]ware is scheduled for
next Friday at 11:00 a.m. in the conference room.

A lunch will follow the demonstration. We hope you can attend.

Yours truly,

Insert   HP DeskJet 500 (Win)   Select October 10, 1994   12:36PM Pg 1 Ln 1" Pos 5.08"

◆ The **Pages** dialog
box appears.

9 Move the mouse ⬚ over
the pages that you want to
display the header or footer
(example: **Every Page**) and
then press the left button.

VIEW HEADERS OR FOOTERS

You can use 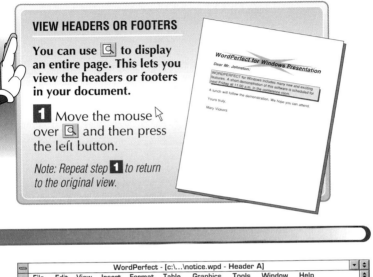 to display an entire page. This lets you view the headers or footers in your document.

1 Move the mouse ⌖ over ⬚ and then press the left button.

*Note: Repeat step **1** to return to the original view.*

WordPerfect - [c:\...\notice.wpd - Header A]

File   Edit   View   Insert   Format   Table   Graphics   Tools   Window   Help

Arial   ▾ 16 pt ▾ Styles   ▾ Left   ▾ 1.0   ▾ Tables   ▾ Columns   ▾ 100% ▾

Number ▾   Insert Line   Pages...   Distance...   Next   Previous   Close

WordPerfect f

Dear Mr. Joh

Pages
Place On
◯ Odd Pages
◯ Even Pages
◉ Every Page

OK
Cancel
Help

WORDPERFE   new and exciting features. A short demonstration of this software is scheduled for next Friday at 11:00 a.m. in the conference room.

A lunch will follow the demonstration. We hope you can attend.

Yours truly,

Insert   HP DeskJet 500 (Win)   Select   October 10, 1994   12:37PM   Pg 1 Ln 1" Pos 5.08"

---

10 Move the mouse ⌖ over **OK** and then press the left button.

11 Move the mouse ⌖ over **Close** and then press the left button.

ADD FOOTNOTES

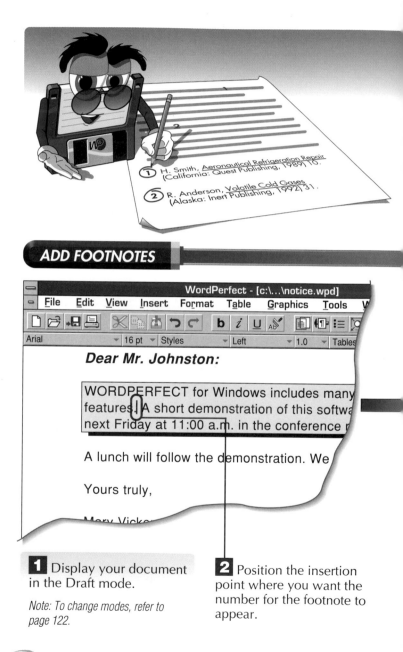

ADD FOOTNOTES

Dear Mr. Johnston:

WORDPERFECT for Windows includes many features. A short demonstration of this softwa next Friday at 11:00 a.m. in the conference r

A lunch will follow the demonstration. We

Yours truly,

Mary Vick

1 Display your document in the Draft mode.

Note: To change modes, refer to page 122.

2 Position the insertion point where you want the number for the footnote to appear.

You can add
a footnote to the
bottom of a page
to provide additional
information about
text in your
document.

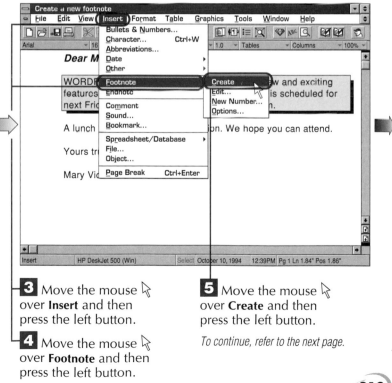

3 Move the mouse ⌖ over **Insert** and then press the left button.

4 Move the mouse ⌖ over **Footnote** and then press the left button.

5 Move the mouse ⌖ over **Create** and then press the left button.

To continue, refer to the next page.

213

ADD FOOTNOTES

Close the Footnote/Endnote feature bar

File Edit View Insert Format Table Graphics Tools Window Help

Arial — 16 pt — Styles — Left — 1.0 — Tables — Columns — 100%

Note Number   Next   Previous   Close

[1] WordPerfect will automatically adjust the text in your document to fit the footnote on the correct page.

Insert   HP DeskJet 500 (Win)   Select October 10, 1994   12:40PM Pg 1 Ln 1.25" Pos 5.69"

6 Type the footnote text.

Note: To change the design and size of the text, refer to page 150.

7 Move the mouse ⊳ over **Close** and then press the left button.

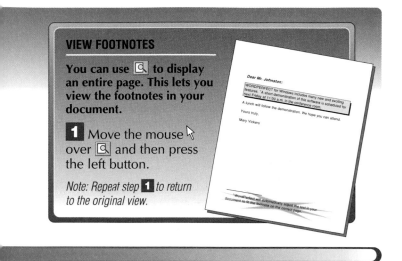

VIEW FOOTNOTES

You can use 🔍 to display an entire page. This lets you view the footnotes in your document.

1 Move the mouse ⟋ over 🔍 and then press the left button.

Note: Repeat step 1 to return to the original view.

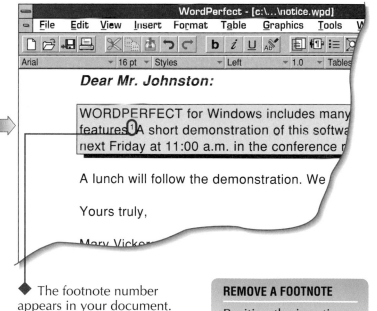

◆ The footnote number appears in your document.

REMOVE A FOOTNOTE

Position the insertion point to the right of the footnote number and then press **+Backspace**.

You can create a table to organize the information in your document.

CREATE A TABLE

Click and drag to create a table

File Edit View Insert Format Table Graphics Tools Window Help

Times New Roman 12 pt Styles Left 1.0 Tables Columns 100%

Insert   HP DeskJet 500 (Win)   Select October 10, 1994   12:53PM Pg 1 Ln 1" Pos 1"

1 Position the insertion point where you want the table to appear in your document.

Note: This example adds a table to a new document. To create a new document, refer to page 128.

2 Move the mouse ⅄ over this box.

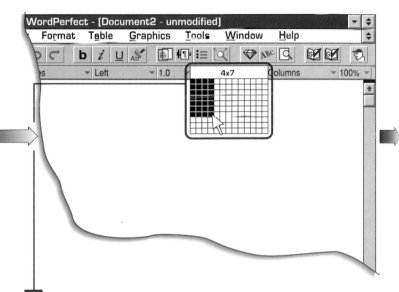

3 Press and hold down the left button as you move the mouse ⯈ over the table size you want to create (example: **4x7**).

To continue, refer to the next page.

CREATE A TABLE

A table consists of columns, rows and cells.

Tap Tap Tap

CREATE A TABLE (CONTINUED)

4 Release the left button and the table appears.

◆ The **Tables** toolbar appears when the insertion point is in the table.

218

◆ A **column** is a vertical line of boxes.

◆ A **row** is a horizontal line of boxes.

◆ A **cell** is one box in a table.

Cell D7				

File Edit View Insert Format Table Graphics Tools Window Help

Arial   ▾ 16 pt ▾ Styles   ▾ Left   ▾ 1.0 ▾ Table   ▾ Columns   ▾ 100% ▾

SALES			
	January	February	March
Jacob	$875	$726	$845
Cathy	$658	$589	$697
Megan	$946	$963	$831
David	$876	$649	$954
Total	$3355	$2927	$3327

TABLE A Cell D7 = 3 HP DeskJet 500 (Win)   Select October 10, 1994   12:56PM Pg 1 Ln 3.34" Pos 6.58"

Enter Text in a Table

5 Move the mouse I over the cell where you want to enter text and then press the left button. Then type the text.

6 Repeat step **5** until you have entered all the text.

Note: To change the font for the entire table, refer to page 150.

CHANGE COLUMN WIDTH

You can change the width of columns to better display the information in your table.

CHANGE COLUMN WIDTH

Drag to adjust column widths - Ctrl+< and Ctrl+>

File   Edit   View   Insert   Format   Table   Graphics   Tools   Window   Help

Arial   16 pt   Styles   Left   1.0   Table   Columns   100%

SALES			
	January	February	March
Jacob	$875	$726	$845
Cathy	$658	$589	$697
Megan	$946	$963	$831
David	$876	$649	$954
Total	$3355	$2927	$3327

Position: 1.94 "

1 Move the mouse I over the left or right edge of the column you want to adjust and I changes to ✛.

2 Press and hold down the left button as you drag the edge of the column to a new position.

◆ A dotted line indicates the new position.

220

WordPerfect - [Document2]

File Edit View Insert Format Table Graphics Tools Window Help

Arial   16 pt   Styles   Left   1.0   Table   Columns   100%

SALES			
	January	February	March
Jacob	$875	$726	$845
Cathy	$658	$589	$697
Megan	$946	$963	$831
David	$876	$649	$954
Total	$3355	$2927	$3327

TABLE A Cell A1   HP DeskJet 500 (Win)   Select October 10, 1994   12:58PM Pg 1 Ln 1.08" Pos 1.79"

3 Release the button
and the new column
width appears.

SELECT CELLS

Cell A3			
SALES			
	January	February	March
Jacob	$875	$726	$845
Cathy	$658	$589	$697
Megan	$946	$963	$831
David	$876	$649	$954
Total	$3355	$2927	$3327

TABLE A Cell A3 | HP DeskJet 500 (Win) | Select October 10, 1994 | 12:59PM Pg 1 Ln 1.84" Pos 1.08"

Select a Cell

1 Move the mouse I next to the left edge of the cell (I changes to ⇦) and then press the left button.

Note: To deselect cells, move the mouse I outside the selected area and then press the left button.

222

> Before you can make changes to your table, you must select the cells you want to modify. Selected cells appear highlighted on your screen.

Cell D6				
File	Edit	View	Insert	Format	Table	Graphics	Tools	Window	Help

Arial — 16 pt — Styles — Left — 1.0 — Table — Columns — 100%

SALES			
	January	February	March
Jacob	$875	$726	$845
Cathy	$658	$589	$697
Megan	$946	$963	$831
David	$876	$649	$954
Total	$3355	$2927	$3327

TABLE A Cell D6 = $ HP DeskJet 500 (Win)   Select   October 10, 1994   1:00PM   Pg 1 Ln 2.97" Pos 6.45"

Select Several Cells

1 Move the mouse I over the first cell you want to select and then press and hold down the left button.

2 Still holding down the button, move the mouse ⇐ until you highlight all the cells you want to select. Then release the button.

223

ADD A ROW OR COLUMN

ADD A ROW OR COLUMN

```
Insert new rows or columns
File   Edit   View   Insert   Format   Table   Graphics   Tools   Window   Help
```

Menu showing Table menu options:
- Create...   F12
- Format...   Ctrl+F12
- Number Type...   Alt+F12
- Expert...
- Lines/Fill...   Shift+F12
- Insert...
- Delete...
- Join   ▶
- Split   ▶
- Names...
- Calculate...
- Copy Formula...
- Data Fill   Ctrl+Shift+F12
- Sum   Ctrl+=
- Cell Formula Entry
- Formula Bar

Arial   ▼ 16 pt ▼ Styles   ▼ Columns   ▼ 100% ▼

SALES			
	Januar		March
Jacob	$875		$845
Cathy	$658		$697
Megan	$946		$831
David	$876		$954
Total	$3355	$2927	$3327

```
TABLE A Cell A3   HP DeskJet 500 (Win)   Select October 10, 1994   1:01PM Pg 1 Ln 1.84" Pos 1.08"
```

1 Position the insertion point where you want to add a row or column.

2 Move the mouse ⤹ over **Table** and then press the left button.

3 Move the mouse ⤹ over **Insert** and then press the left button.

224

You can add
a row or column
to your table if you
want to insert new
information.

WordPerfect - [Document2]

File   Edit   View   Insert   Format   Table   Graphics   Tools   Window   Help

Arial   16 pt   Styles   Left   1.0   Table   Columns   100%

Insert Columns/Rows

Table Size
Columns: 4
Rows: 7

OK
Cancel
Help

Insert
○ Columns: 1
● Rows: 1

Placement
● Before
○ After

SALES

	March
Jacob	$845
Cathy	$697
Megan	$831
David	$954
Total	$3327

TABLE A Cell A3   HP DeskJet 500 (Win)   Select   October 10, 1994   1:02PM   Pg 1 Ln 1.84" Pos 1.08"

◆ The **Insert Columns/Rows** dialog box appears.

4 To add a row, move the mouse ⓡ over **Rows:** and then press the left button.

◆ To add a column, move the mouse ⓡ over **Columns:** and then press the left button.

To continue, refer to the next page.

225

ADD A ROW OR COLUMN (CONTINUED)

WordPerfect - [Document2]

File Edit View Insert Format Table Graphics Tools Window Help

Arial   16 pt   Styles   Left   1.0   Table   Columns   100%

Insert Columns/Rows

Table Size
Columns: 4
Rows: 7

[OK]
[Cancel]
[Help]

Insert
○ Columns: 1
● Rows: 1

Placement
● Before
○ After

SALES		March
Jacob		$845
Cathy		$697
Megan		$831
David		$954
Total		$3327

TABLE A Cell A3   HP DeskJet 500 (Win)   Select   October 10, 1994   1:03PM   Pg 1 Ln 1.84" Pos 1.08"

5 Move the mouse ⏳ over the placement option you want to use and then press the left button.

*Note: **Before** places the new row or column before the cell containing the insertion point. **After** places the new row or column after the cell containing the insertion point.*

6 Move the mouse ⏳ over **OK** and then press the left button.

226

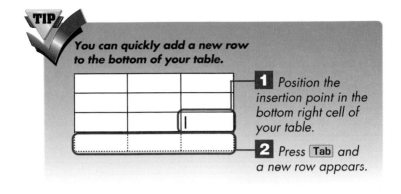

TIP

You can quickly add a new row to the bottom of your table.

1 Position the insertion point in the bottom right cell of your table.

2 Press **Tab** and a new row appears.

```
                    WordPerfect - [Document2]
 File   Edit   View   Insert   Format   Table   Graphics   Tools   Window   Help

Arial          16 pt    Styles         Left        1.0    Table         Columns      100%
```

SALES			
	January	February	March
Jacob	$875	$726	$845
Cathy	$658	$589	$697
Megan	$946	$963	$831
David	$876	$649	$954
Total	$3355	$2927	$3327

```
TABLE A Cell A3   HP DeskJet 500 (Win)      Select   October 10, 1994   1:04PM   Pg 1 Ln 1.84" Pos 1.08"
```

◆ The new row or column appears.

DELETE A ROW
OR COLUMN

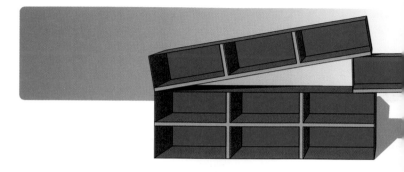

Cell D3				
File	Edit	View	Insert	Format	Table	Graphics	Tools	Window	Help

Arial — 16 pt — Styles — Left — 1.0 — Table — Columns — 100%

SALES			
	January	February	March
			←
Jacob	$875	$726	$845
Cathy	$658	$589	$697
Megan	$946	$963	$831
David	$876	$649	$954
Total	$3355	$2927	$3327

TABLE A Cell D3 | HP DeskJet 500 (Win) | Select October 10, 1994 | 1:05PM Pg 1 Ln 1.84" Pos 5.96"

1 Select all the cells in the row or column you want to delete.

Note: To select cells, refer to page 222.

2 Press **Delete** on your keyboard.

228

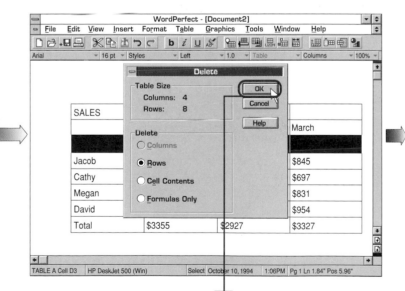

◆ The **Delete** dialog box appears.

3 To delete the row or column you selected, move the mouse ▷ over **OK** and then press the left button.

To continue, refer to the next page.

DELETE A ROW OR COLUMN

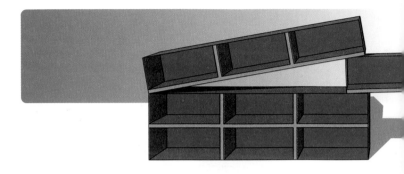

WordPerfect - [Document2]

File Edit View Insert Format Table Graphics Tools Window Help

Arial   16 pt   Styles   Left   1.0   Table   Columns   100%

SALES			
	January	February	March
Jacob	$875	$726	$845
Cathy	$658	$589	$697
Megan	$946	$963	$831
David	$876	$649	$954
Total	$3355	$2927	$3327

TABLE A Cell D3 = 8 HP DeskJet 500 (Win)   Select October 10, 1994   1:07PM Pg 1 Ln 1.84" Pos 5.96"

◆ The row or column disappears.

230

When you delete a row or column from your table, the remaining rows or columns move to fill the empty space.

DELETE A TABLE

```
┌─────────────────────────────────────────────┐
│ ▬           Delete Table                     │
│ ┌─ Delete ────────────────────┐   ┌────────┐ │
│ │ ● Entire Table              │   │   OK   │ │
│ │ ○ Table Contents            │   └────────┘ │
│ │ ○ Formulas Only             │   ┌────────┐ │
│ │ ○ Table Structure (leave text)│ │ Cancel │ │
│ │ ○ Convert to Merge Data File│   └────────┘ │
│ │ ○ Convert to Merge Data File│   ┌────────┐ │
│ │   (first row becomes field names)││ Help  │ │
│ │                             │   └────────┘ │
│ └─────────────────────────────┘             │
└─────────────────────────────────────────────┘
```

1 Select all the cells in the table you want to delete.

Note: To select cells, refer to page 222.

2 Press Delete and the **Delete Table** dialog box appears.

3 Move the mouse ⌖ over **OK** and then press the left button.

231

JOIN CELLS

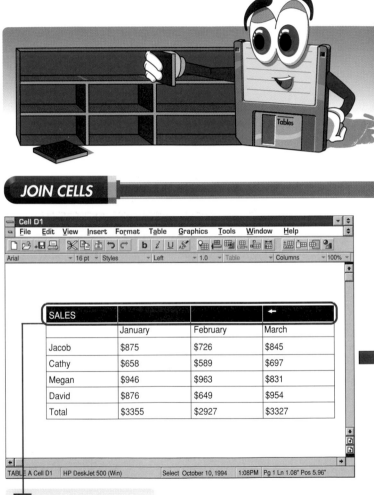

1 Select the cells you want to join.

Note: To select cells, refer to page 222.

You can combine two or more cells in your table to make one large cell.

Format	Table	Graphics	Tools	Window	Help

Create...   F12

Format...   Ctrl+F12
Number Type... Alt+F12
Expert...
Lines/Fill...   Shift+F12

Insert...
Delete...
Join ▶
Split ▶

Names...
Calculate...
Copy Formula...
Data Fill Ctrl+Shift+F12

~ Columns ~ 100% ~

anuar	March
75	$845
	$697
	$831

2 Move the mouse ⅄ over **Table** and then press the left button.

3 Move the mouse ⅄ over **Join** and then press the left button.

To continue, refer to the next page.

JOIN CELLS

m one cell

| Format | Table | Graphics | Tools | Window | Help |

Create...   F12

Format...   Ctrl+F12   Columns   100%
Number Type...   Alt+F12
Expert...
Lines/Fill...   Shift+F12

Insert...
Delete...

Join   Cell
Split   Table

Names...
Calculate...
Copy Formula...
Data Fill   Ctrl+Shift+F12

anuar   March

75             $845

               $697

               $831

4 Move the mouse ↖ over **Cell** and then press the left button.

Joining cells
is useful when
you want to display
a title at the top of
your table.

WordPerfect - [Document2]

File Edit View Insert Format Table Graphics Tools Window Help

Arial   16 pt Styles   Left   1.0   Table   Columns   100%

SALES			
	January	February	March
Jacob	$875	$726	$845
Cathy	$658	$589	$697
Megan	$946	$963	$831
David	$876	$649	$954
Total	$3355	$2927	$3327

TABLE A Cell A1 HP DeskJet 500 (Win) Select October 10, 1994 1:11PM Pg 1 Ln 1.08" Pos 1.08"

◆ The cells are joined.

USING THE TABLE EXPERT

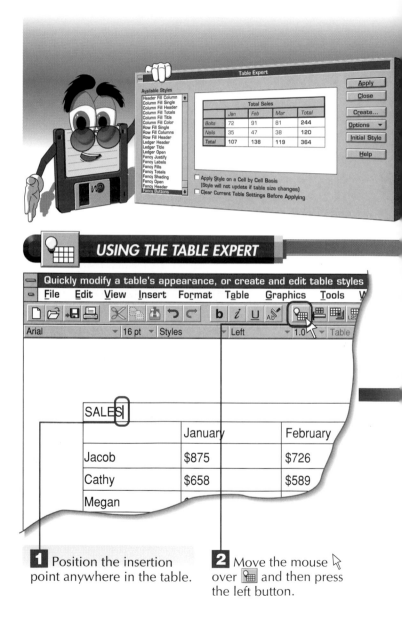

USING THE TABLE EXPERT

Quickly modify a table's appearance, or create and edit table styles

| File | Edit | View | Insert | Format | Table | Graphics | Tools | W |

Arial ▼ 16 pt ▼ Styles ▼ Left ▼ 1.0 ▼ Table

SALES		
	January	February
Jacob	$875	$726
Cathy	$658	$589
Megan		

1 Position the insertion point anywhere in the table.

2 Move the mouse ⬚ over 🎞 and then press the left button.

236

You can save time by using the Table Expert feature to enhance the appearance of your table.

WordPerfect - [Document2]

File   Edit   View   Insert   Format   Table   Graphics   Tools   Window   Help

Table Expert

Available Styles

<None>
No Lines Single
No Lines No Border
No Lines Columns
No Lines Header
No Lines Totals
No Lines Separator
Single Lines
Single Double Border
Single Bold Title
Single No Border
Single Underlined
Single Open
Double Border Header
Double Border Bold
Double Border Title
Double Border Mixed
Double Border Totals
Header Fill Single
Header Fill Title

Apply
Close
Create...
Options ▼
Initial Style
Help

	Jan	Feb	Mar	Total
Nuts	72	91	81	244
Bolts	35	47	38	120
Nails	77	98	89	264
Total	184	236	208	628

☐ Apply Style on a Cell by Cell Basis
   (Style will not update if table size changes)
☐ Clear Current Table Settings Before Applying

TABLE A Cell A1   HP DeskJet 500 (Win)   Select   October 10, 1994   1:13 PM   Pg 1 Ln 1.08" Pos 1.79"

◆ The **Table Expert** dialog box appears.

◆ This area displays a list of the available table designs.

◆ This area displays a sample of the highlighted table design.

To continue, refer to the next page.

USING THE TABLE EXPERT

USING THE TABLE EXPERT (CONTINUED)

WordPerfect - [Document2]

File   Edit   View   Insert   Format   Table   Graphics   Tools   Window   Help

Table Expert

Available Styles

Header Fill Column
Column Fill Single
Column Fill Header
Column Fill Totals
Column Fill Title
Column Fill Color
Row Fill Single
Row Fill Columns
Row Fill Header
Ledger Header
Ledger Title
Ledger Open
Fancy Justify
Fancy Labels
Fancy Fills
Fancy Totals
Fancy Shading
Fancy Open
Fancy Header
Fancy Buttons

Apply
Close
Create...
Options
Initial Style
Help

	Total Sales			
	Jan	Feb	Mar	Total
Bolts	72	91	81	244
Nails	35	47	38	120
Total	107	138	119	364

☐ Apply Style on a Cell by Cell Basis
(Style will not update if table size changes)
☐ Clear Current Table Settings Before Applying

TABLE A Cell A1   HP DeskJet 500 (Win)   Select October 10, 1994   1:14 PM   Pg 1 Ln 1.08" Pos 1.79"

3 Press ↓ or ↑ on your keyboard until this area displays the design you want to use (example: **Fancy Buttons**).

4 Move the mouse over **Apply** and then press the left button.

238

> WordPerfect
> lets you select
> from forty table
> designs.

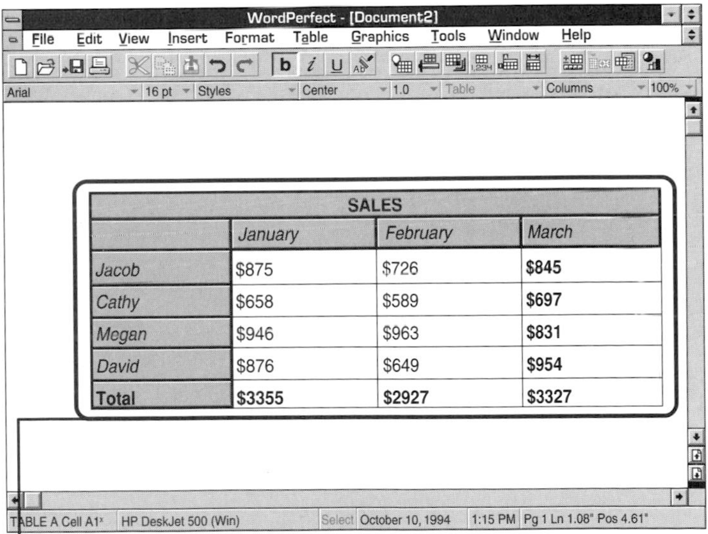

◆ WordPerfect applies
the design you selected
to the table.

INDEX

INDEX

The fun & easy way to learn about computers and more!

Windows 3.1 For Dummies,™ 2nd Edition
by Andy Rathbone

ISBN: 1-56884-182-5
$16.95 USA/$22.95 Canada

MORE Windows For Dummies™
by Andy Rathbone

ISBN: 1-56884-048-9
$19.95 USA/$26.95 Canada

Personal Finance For Dummies™
by Eric Tyson

ISBN: 1-56884-150-7
$16.95 USA/$22.95 Canada

PCs For Dummies,™ 2nd Edition
by Dan Gookin & Andy Rathbone

ISBN: 1-56884-078-0
$16.95 USA/$22.95 Canada

ORDER FORM

TRADE & INDIVIDUAL ORDERS

Phone: **(800) 762-2974**
or **(317) 895-5200**
(8 a.m.–6 p.m., CST, weekdays)
FAX : **(317) 895-5298**

IDG BOOKS

CORPORATE ORDERS FOR INTROGRAPHIC BOOKS

Phone: **(800) 469-6616** *ext.* **206**
(8 a.m.–5 p.m., EST, weekdays)
FAX : **(905) 890-9434**

Qty	ISBN	Title	Price	Total

Shipping & Handling Charges

	Description	First book	Each add'l. book	Total
Domestic	Normal	$4.50	$1.50	$
	Two Day Air	$8.50	$2.50	$
	Overnight	$18.00	$3.00	$
International	Surface	$8.00	$8.00	$
	Airmail	$16.00	$16.00	$
	DHL Air	$17.00	$17.00	$

Subtotal _____

*CA residents add
applicable sales tax* _____

IN, MA and MD
residents add
5% sales tax _____

IL residents add
6.25% sales tax _____

RI residents add
7% sales tax _____

TX residents add
8.25% sales tax _____

Shipping _____

Total _____

Ship to:

Name _____

Address_____

Company _____

City/State/Zip _____

Daytime Phone_____

Payment: ☐ Check to IDG Books (US Funds Only)
      ☐ Visa ☐ Mastercard ☐ American Express

Card # _____ Exp. _____

Signature_____

IDG Books Education Group
Jim Kelly, Director of Education Sales – 9 Village Circle, Ste. 450, Westlake, TX 76262
800-434-2086 Phone • 817-430-5852 Fax • 8:30-5:00 CST